THE PATTERN MAKING PRIMER

First edition for North America and the Philippines published
in 2012 by Barron's Educational Series, Inc.

All inquiries should be addressed to:
Barron's Educational Series, Inc.
250 Wireless Boulevard, Hauppauge, New York 11788

www.barronseduc.com

ISBN-13: 978-1-4380-0083-1

Library of Congress Control No.: 2011943766

Printed in China

9 8 7 6 5 4 3 2 1

Art Director: Emily Portnoi
Design concept: Emily Portnoi
Artwork and layout: Rebecca Stephenson
Commissioning Editor: Isheeta Mustafi
Illustrations: Jo Barnfield

THE PATTERN MAKING PRIMER

ALL YOU NEED TO KNOW ABOUT DESIGNING, ADAPTING & CUSTOMIZING SEWING PATTERNS

JO BARNFIELD & ANDREW RICHARDS

BARRON'S

CONTENTS

③

PATTERN DEVELOPMENT 104

④

THE DESIGNER MAKER 174

INTRODUCTION

PATTERN ANNOTATIONS

Proper pattern annotation is the main form of communication on the pattern piece; it is vital that it is clear and informative. For the sewing machinist it assures that the garment can be properly constructed, that each piece of a pattern is present, and that seam allowances, notches, and dart positions are in place and are accurate.

MARKING LINES

Some of the main information on the pattern indicates the following:

- The cut line and stitch line. These denote the edges of the allowance needed to seam the garment. Tracing the pattern off to the stitch line gives a nett pattern, which is best used if the pattern needs to be altered.
- Grainline. The grainline has arrows at either end to show direction. (NB: a red, arrowed line is used in this book to indicate the grainline.)
- Center front (CF) and center back (CB).
- The main horizontal body measurement lines, such as waist, hip, bust (including the bust point).
- "Place on fold" bracket, indicating that the pattern piece should be placed on to folded fabric to create a mirrored piece once cut.
- Cut right side up (Cut RSU) or occasionally cut wrong side up (Cut WSU). Right side and wrong side may be abbreviated as RS and WS respectively.
- Left-hand side (LHS) and right-hand side (RHS).
- Darts and pocket positions indicated by a punched drill hole in the pattern.
- Pleat direction marked with an arrow from fold to end position.
- Interior cut lines such as for a placket opening on a sleeve.
- Fold lines such as on a button stand or pleat.
- Roll lines such as the soft roll line of a collar or break line of a rever.
- Hemline.
- Fastening positions for buttons and buttonholes, zippers, and so on.

ANNOTATION SHOULD INCLUDE:

- The garment name or style code, e.g., Raglan Sleeve Raincoat.
- The garment grade, e.g., size 12.
- The pattern piece, e.g., sleeve, pocket flap.
- The number of the piece, e.g., piece 2 of 8.
- An explanation for the cutter, e.g., cut 1 pair self and fusing, cut on fold, etc.
- Seam allowance, e.g., $\frac{3}{8}$in (1cm) SA, Nett, etc.
- The date, or the version number.

If you are working in a team, it is also helpful to include the name or initials of the pattern designer who created the pattern.

COMMON PATTERN ANNOTATION

NAME	DESCRIPTION	ANNOTATION
Pattern adjustment lines	Two parallel lines indicate lengthening or shortening position.	
Grainline	Indicate the direction the pattern piece should be laid on to fabric. A colored line has been used throughout this book to indicate grain direction.	
Cut on fold	Denotes pattern piece that should be cut on a folded piece of fabric.	
Cut line (single size)	Indicates the cut line.	
Cut line (multisize)	A commercial dressmaking pattern contains multiple sizes on one tissue; in industry this is called a graded nest. This line may be solid or dashed.	
Stitch line	Not all commercial patterns indicate the stitch line, especially ones that contain multiple sizes.	
Notches	Triangle-shaped marks that indicate positions on individual seams that need to be lined up during construction. A double triangle indicates a back pattern piece.	
Pleat symbols	Indicate pleat position and pleat fold direction.	
Button position	Marks the placement of buttons.	
Buttonhole position	Marks the placement of buttonholes.	
Drill hole	Can indicate precise matching or construction points.	

1

THE BASICS

CHAPTER 1:
TOOLS, SUPPLIES, AND EQUIPMENT

It is important to understand the tools of the pattern-cutting trade before you start. Some are essential (such as a measuring tape) or multifunctional (such as Patternmaster) and you will use them constantly; others have a specific use (e.g., a pattern notcher) and you will need them less often. These tools can be accumulated over time, and you may form your own equipment preferences as you work.

PATTERN-CUTTING EQUIPMENT

ESSENTIAL ITEMS

These items are essential if you want to create professional patterns.

- **Tape measure:** Used for taking body measurements and measuring curves on pattern pieces. (1)

- **Metal ruler:** A yard- or meter-length metal ruler keeps a true straight line. A smaller 12in (30cm) metal ruler is also useful. (2)

- **Set square:** This ensures that lines run true at 90 degrees on a pattern. (3)

- **French curves:** Use for forming smaller curves such as collars. (4)

- **Clicker's awl:** This tool can be used to make small holes in pattern pieces. It can also be used to help pivot darts accurately. (5)

- **Tracing wheel:** This is used to trace through both paper and fabric to mark lines and positions with a continuous line of small pinpricks on a piece of paper underneath. (6)

- **Pattern paper and card:** These are also essential for creating pattern drafts and "working" (in process) patterns. Pattern paper is very thin and can be traced through, while pattern card is more hardwearing (not shown).

ALSO USEFUL

The following items may be useful in pattern-cutting, but are not so fundamental.

- Pattern notcher (7)
- Patternmaster (8)
- Hip curve (9)
- Flexi curve (10)
- T-square (11)
- Pattern drill (12)
- Shoben marking tape or style tape (13)
- Dress form (not shown)

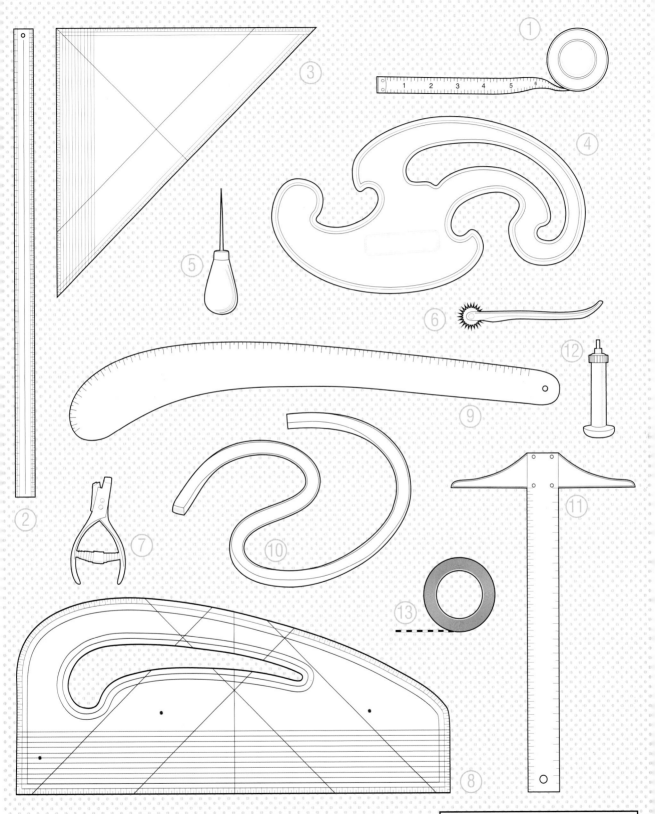

THE BASICS

Tools, supplies, and equipment

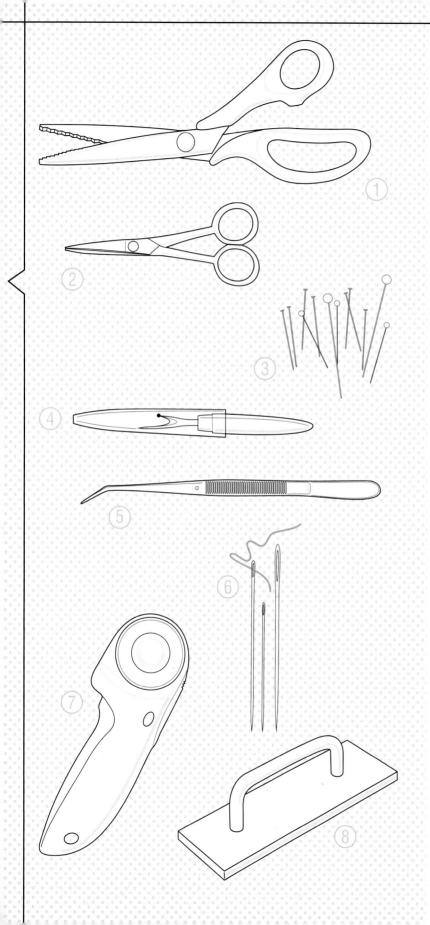

GARMENT CONSTRUCTION EQUIPMENT

ESSENTIAL ITEMS

The following are essential in the process of garment construction.

- **Shears:** Large scissors with blades over 6in (15cm) long. (1)

- **Embroidery scissors:** Small precision scissors for cutting to exact points and trimming threads. (2)

- **Pins:** These hold garment sections in position for seaming, and pattern to paper when cutting out. (3)

- **Seam ripper:** Used to quickly undo an incorrect seam. (4)

- **Tweezers:** A precision tool whose many purposes include threading machinery. (5)

- **Hand-sewing needles:** These include crewels (embroidery needles), sharps (short hand-sewing needles), betweens, and blunts (shorter needles used by tailors on heavy fabrics). (6)

- **Lint brush:** This will help to raise pile on fabrics, as well as removing fluff (not shown).

ALSO USEFUL

- Rotary cutter (7)
- Fabric weights (8)
- Fabric sealant (not shown)

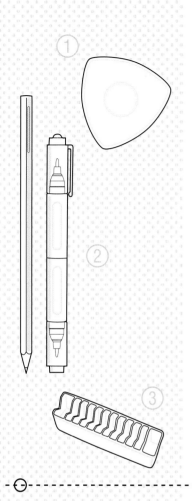

MARKING TOOLS

ESSENTIAL ITEMS

Note that all marks on fabric should be temporary; test these methods before use on fabric to find the most suitable.

- **Tailor's chalk:** This is available in many colors, and is one of the most traditional methods used to create temporary marks on the fabric. These chalks can blunt quickly; however, there are tools available that use chalk dust to produce continuous, fine, sharp chalk lines. (1)

- **Clothmarking pencils and pens:** A chalk pencil can be quite waxy and not easily removed from fabric. Clothmarking pens use ink that either disappears within 24 hours or can be removed with water. They are commonly double-ended with an ink-removal solution at the other end if you want to erase markings immediately. (2)

- **Thread tracing:** This is another way of marking fabric: a type of running stitch that is visible as a line on both sides of the fabric (not shown).

ALSO USEFUL
- Chalk sharpener (3)

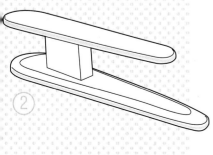

PRESSING TOOLS

Pressing is fundamental to a well-made garment.

- **Press cloth:** A press cloth is a piece of fabric, usually cotton, that you can put over fabric when pressing so the iron does not damage the fabric (not shown).

- **Ham:** Derived from the traditional word for buttocks, the tailor's ham is used to press three-dimensional shapes; for example, in bust or hip shaping. (1)

- **Sleeve board:** This is a narrow padded board for pressing sleeves and sleeveheads, as well as other tubular garment shapes that cannot be pressed flat on the ironing board. (2)

- **Iron cleaner:** A metal cleaner used for cleaning the metal base of an iron (not shown).

THE BASICS
Tools, supplies, and equipment

USING A SEWING MACHINE

Domestic sewing machines usually serve a variety of purposes, whereas machines used in industry are often specific to one purpose (for example, an overlock machine).

ESSENTIAL FEATURES

The following are the essential considerations when using a domestic sewing machine for putting together your designs.

- **Sewing machine:** This is an all-purpose machine, with various stitches for seams, decorative embroidery stitches, and buttonholes. Designed for the home user, it is unsuitable for heavy industrial use. (1)

- **Machine needles:** The type and weight of fabric dictates which needle you should use. A standard needle has a pointed tip and is suitable for most wovens; leather needles have a tip more similar to a blade, to cut into the material rather than to pierce it; jersey/knit needles have a ballpoint, or rounded head, so as not to damage or snag the knit. Each of these needles is available in many sizes, with finer needles more suitable for lightweight fabrics, and thicker needles for heavier ones. (2)

- **Machine threads:** Threads are available in many weights and fiber compositions. The type of thread used is determined both by the weight of the fabric and its purpose, whether for seaming or topstitching. (3)

- **Bulk threads:** Bulk threads are a loosely twisted polyester thread; used for an overlock machine, this type of thread gives a flat appearance (not shown).

MACHINE FEET

Depending on the make and model of your machine, a range of feet is available:

- **Plain foot:** For most general machine-stitching. (4)

- **Teflon foot:** A Teflon-coated plastic foot for use on slippery fabrics and some leathers. (5)

- **Velvet foot:** A narrow foot for fabrics with a heavy pile such as velvet and velour. (6)

- **Zipper feet:** These are available in left- and right-side versions. (7)

- **Invisible/concealed zipper foot:** A small foot with grooved guides for attaching invisible or concealed zippers. (8)

ALSO USEFUL

- A narrow foot is able to stitch closely to an edge. Used mostly for attaching plain zippers, but also for piping (not shown).

- Binding attachments are handy for producing bound seams and hems in one step (not shown).

- Ruffler feet are useful for creating an even gather (not shown).

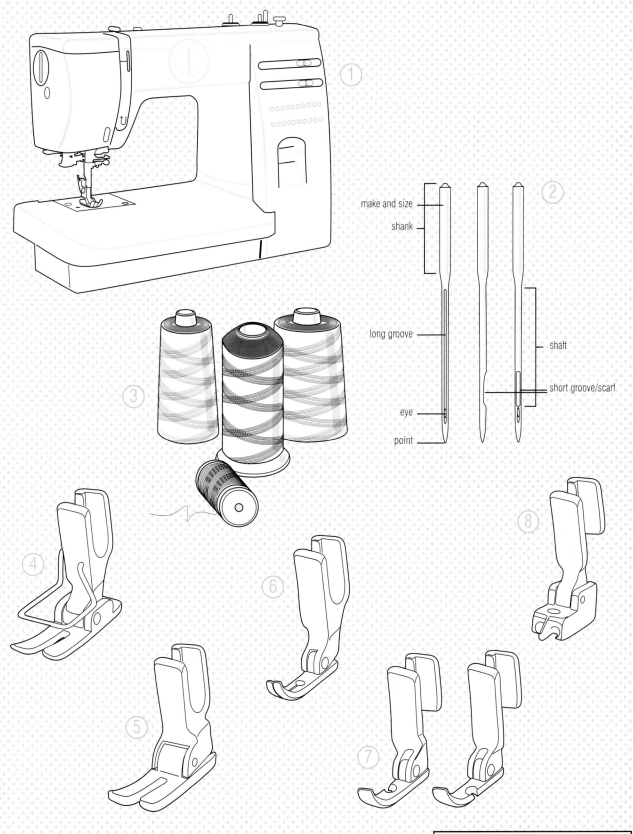

make and size

shank

long groove

shaft

short groove/scarf

eye

point

THE BASICS

Tools, supplies, and equipment

CHAPTER 2: FUNDAMENTALS OF A GARMENT

SEAMS

Seams are lines of stitching that join together individual garment sections. The type of seam used is determined by elements such as fabric (its thickness, whether it has stretch, and so on); the desired look (a certain seam may help to impart a certain feel, such as a machine-felled seam for workwear or jeans); and the location of the seam (whether a stronger, more durable seam is most appropriate).

PREPARING TO SEW SEAMS

Check the machine tension on a scrap of the fabric before you sew. The stitch should be flat and regular, not puckered or loopy. Sewing problems can stem from incorrect tension, machine threading, stitch length, needle size, or a blunt or bent needle.

A seam guide can be used to keep a constant, accurate seam width. However, with experience you will become less reliant on it and be able to visualize a precise seam allowance in relation to the foot width.

With certain exceptions, each seam must be backstitched by sewing back and forth for a couple of stitches at the start and finish of the seam. This secures the seam and prevents it from opening up.

An alternative to backstitching is to tie off the threads at both ends. This is more of a couture finish, but there are times when this is appropriate for certain fabrics.

At the end of each seam, threads must be trimmed, and the seam pressed in preparation for the next stage. A seam should be almost invisible when sewn; however, decorative seaming and topstitching can be used to enhance style lines within a garment.

MATCHING THE THREAD

Use the correct thread for the fabric that you are using, matching it as closely as possible to the fabric color. If a perfect match cannot be found, go for a slightly lighter tone, as the thread will tend to look darker when the seam is constructed. You should also consider matching thread for appropriate weight and fiber content.

MATCHING SEAMS

Seams must be matched accurately; there are ways to ensure this,
as explained below.

PINNING

Pins are available in many types and thicknesses. It is important to choose
an appropriate pin size for the fabric used, so it does not leave pinholes that
cannot be removed. Certain materials, such as leather, PVC, or waxed or
coated fabrics, cannot be pinned for this reason; paperclips can be used
instead, or take care to pin just within the seam allowance, so that any pin
marks will not show.

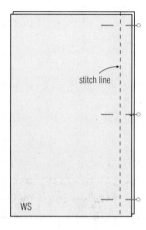

stitch line

WS

When pinning, secure pieces together at each end first, then at notches
and center, and lastly between these points at 3–4in (7.5–10cm) intervals.
Too many pins can hinder construction. Take care to remove pins while
you are sewing; sewing over a pin can result in either a broken needle
or an irregular stitch line.

It is best to pin across, rather than down, the seam, as this helps to secure
points together more accurately. When trying to match two seams that cross
through one another, match seams at the stitch line and pin 1/2in (1.2cm) on
either side. Pinning here rather than on the seam means that the seams are
less likely to slip on one another, and are more likely to line up precisely.

BASTING

Basting is a form of running stitch, hand-tacked along the stitch line.
It is used to keep sections together temporarily for machine sewing.
The basting stitch is a large stitch usually made in a contrasting color
thread. It is unsecured at either end so that it can be removed easily.

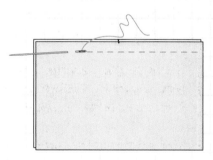

Basting can be more suitable than pins for insetting sleeves, as it gives
an opportunity to check correct balance on the wearer before it is finally
sewn by machine. It can help to more accurately allocate ease within
a seam, such as on a sleevehead.

Basting can also be used to stabilize two layers of fabric that form one
garment section. Here, the stitch is sewn around the edge of the pattern
pieces on the seam allowance.

THE BASICS
Fundamentals of a garment

STAYSTITCHING

Staystitching is a permanent line of stitches made ½in (1.2cm) from the cut edge of a garment section. It helps prevent the piece from stretching and distorting, especially in curved areas such as the neckline or arm hole.

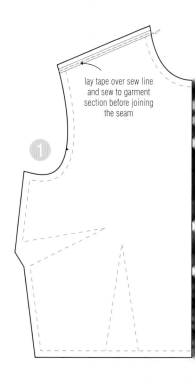

lay tape over sew line and sew to garment section before joining the seam

TAPING SEAMS

A cotton tape sewn onto the seam allowances can be used to support a seam, such as on the shoulder, and stop it from stretching. (1)

DIRECTIONAL SEWING

The direction in which you sew garment sections together plays a key part in construction. Sewing against the grain on a bias or curve can stretch the seam. It is usually best to sew the straightest part of a seam first, such as from hem to waistline on a skirt. Shoulder seams should be constructed from neck to shoulder; side bodice seams from underarm to waist. The exception is fabrics with a pile or nap, which must be sewn upward with the direction of the pile.

TRIMMING SEAMS

Seams can be trimmed back to ³⁄₁₆in (4mm), or graded by trimming back seam allowances to different widths, say ³⁄₁₆ and ⁵⁄₁₆in (4 and 7mm). This removes bulk from the seam allowance and allows seams to lay flatter. Grading ensures that seam allowances do not leave a visible ridge from the right side.

FINISHING SEAMS

If a garment is not lined, seam edges must be finished to prevent them fraying. Some types of seam, such as welt and French seams, are self-neatening—they are finished in the process of construction. However, most need to be neatened through overlocking or binding. Seam finishing should be done as the garment is being made, and before it is sewn to another section.

TYPES OF SEAMS

There are many ways in which two garment parts can be joined, depending on the style and nature of the garment, the fabric type, and the location of the seam. The following are principal seaming techniques.

PLAIN SEAM

A plain seam is the most commonly used method of garment construction. To sew a plain seam:

plain seam, WS

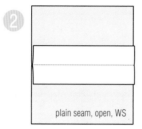

plain seam, open, WS

Right sides of fabric are placed together and a single line of stitch is made on the stitching line (usually ⅜–⅝in/1–1.5cm).

The seam allowances can be splayed and pressed to give an open seam, which gives the flattest finish from the right side.

plain seam, closed, WS

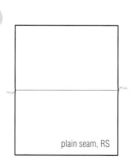

plain seam, RS

The seam allowances can be pressed to one side, giving a closed seam, to create a slightly raised look to one edge.

The completed seam from the right side.

EDGESTITCHED SEAM

Edgestitching is a line of topstitching made close to the edge of a seam. It is both decorative and functional, strengthening the seam and keeping areas such as facings in place. Edgestitching, like topstitching, is usually made in a longer stitch length than that of the seam.

edgestitched seam, open, WS

edgestitched seam, closed, WS

THE BASICS
Fundamentals of a garment

UNDERSTITCHING

Understitching is a single row of edgestitch. It is used to stop profile edges, such as the neckline, arm hole, waistband facing, or lining, from rolling outward. This stitch line is not seen on the outer shell.

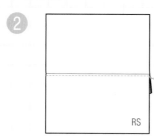

When the seam attaching the garment inner is sewn, lightly press both seam allowances inward toward the facing/lining, then sew the understitch row from the right side of the garment. This catches the seam allowances underneath.

Finished understitching from right side.

SEWING A CORNER SEAM

A corner seam is comprised of a corner piece and an "insert" section. You can press the seam allowances at the corner of both sections, or use a marking pen to act as an "invisible" crease guide to follow when sewing; this helps to indicate the exact pivot point of the corner. To sew a corner seam:

 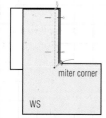

 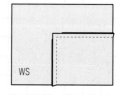

Place the corner piece right side up on the machine, then place the insert section right side down on top of this, matching the stitch lines of one side of the corner (you can't match both edges due to the angle). Stitch from the edge of the seam to the point of the corner. When you reach this point, keep the needle down in the fabric. Dropping down to a smaller stitch length from around 1in (2.5cm) from the corner point can give more accuracy.

With the needle still down, raise the machine foot and snip into the corner section, to within two threads of the needle. Now the corner section will be released and you will be able to turn this section (pivoting on the needle) to meet the other side of the corner insert, to complete the seam.

The finished seam as seen from the wrong side.

INCOMPLETE UNDERSTITCHING

The shape of garment sections—a rever collar or shaped facing, for instance—may dictate that understitching cannot be completed around the whole of a seam.

MITERING CORNERS

Mitering corners cuts away bulk, which if left would stop the points of the corner from turning through properly. Trim the excess at an angle to a point a couple of threads' width away from the stitched corner. Use a pair of tweezers to work the corner through, being careful not to stretch the fabric.

SEWING A CURVED SEAM

Echoing the form of the body, many of the structural seams of a garment are curved, creating contours such as that of the princess line, which takes in bust, waist, and hip shaping. Curved seams incorporate two parts: a concave-curved section, and a convex-curved insert. Before sewing, pieces should be notched correctly at intervals for ease of insertion. To sew a curved seam:

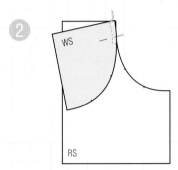

Place the concave piece right sides up on the machine.

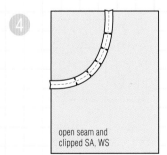

Matching the stitching lines, place the convex piece on top, right side down. Start stitching.

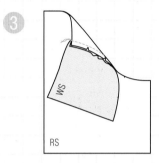

When the curved sections start to diverge, manipulate the concave section to follow the under-section, while keeping this bottom section flat. Although the stitching lines are the same length, the seam edge of the convex curve is longer than the concave. The idea when stitching is to make the concave section fit the shape of the convex section; because of this, the concave edge will frill slightly when stitched. Lowering the stitch length gives greater control when stitching the curve, and a smoother finished seam.

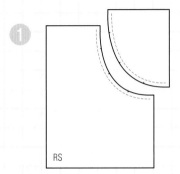

open seam and clipped SA, WS

On curved seams, the seam allowances should be graded. Clipping into the seam allowances of inward (concave) curved seams by $3/16$–$5/16$in (4–7mm) at intervals of 1–1½in (2.5–4cm) can help the seam to open up and lay flat. Notching (not to be confused with pattern notching)—where small triangular sections are clipped out from the seam allowances—can be used on outward (convex) curves. This notching helps remove some of the bulk. Never clip completely to the seam, as this can weaken the seam and lead to the desired curve becoming angular.

FRENCH SEAM

A French seam is a self-neatening seam, originating from the couture ateliers. It is commonly used on very sheer fabrics such as chiffon, fine cotton, and voile. As it uses two lines of stitching, it is also suitable for garments that receive heavy wear, such as nightwear. Due to the extra processes required, the seam is rare within mass industry. It is not recommended for very curved seams. To sew a French seam:

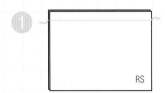

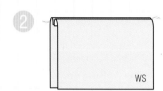

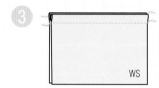

With ½in (1.2cm) seam allowances, place sections wrong sides together with stitch lines matching. Stitch a seam ¼in (6mm) in from the seam edge and trim back to ⅛in (3mm).

Press the seam allowances open, and then fold the seam right sides together.

Stitch another line ¼in (6mm) in from the edge. Open the finished seam and press to one side.

FLAT-FELLED SEAM

This is one of the most hardwearing seams. It is suitable for all fabrics, but is especially common for jeans and heavy cottons. It is a self-neatening seam, where all the raw edges are enclosed, and lends itself to reversible garments and sportswear. A flat-felled seam is constructed from two pieces with differing seam allowances: one has a ¼in (6mm) seam allowance, and the other has a ¾in (2cm) seam allowance that folds around the shorter, to conceal it. To sew a flat-felled seam:

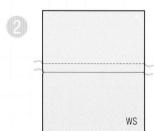

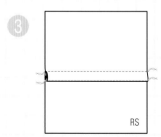

Place the wrong sides together with stitch lines matching; sew along the stitch line.

Press out the seam and fold in the longer edge (right sides together) by ¼in (6mm) and press, enclosing the raw edge of the shorter seam allowance. Edgestitch this folded edge down.

Twin lines of stitching should show from the right side and one row of stitching from the wrong side.

WELT SEAM

The welt seam is very similar in use to a flat-felled seam. It is suitable for medium to heavy fabrics, such as wools, denims, and tweeds. It creates a raised effect, and because of the twin stitch is very durable. A welt seam uses two pieces with different seam allowances, one with ¼in (6mm) and the other with ½in (1.2cm). If the piece is not lined, the longer seam allowance must be overlocked before it is sewn down. To sew a welt seam:

WS

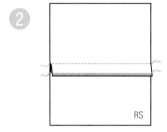

RS

Neaten edge with wider seam allowance and place pieces right sides together with stitch lines matching; sew down the stitch line.

Press the seam, folding the overlocked edge over to cover the shorter raw edge. Turn the fabric to the right side and topstitch so that the longer seam allowance is caught on the underside and the raw edge enclosed.

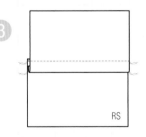

RS

A completed welt seam from the right side. This finish gives a distinctive raised appearance, as seen with welt pockets.

1. Paneled skirt with external seam detailing.

(Photo credit: Bon Marché)

THE BASICS
Fundamentals of a garment

BOUND SEAM

Binding is a way of finishing that encloses the raw fabric edge with a strip of bias-cut fabric, which can be either in the self-fabric or a contrast material. It is a suitable finish for many fabrics, but is often seen in unlined outerwear. Machine feet with binding attachments can be bought for industrial and domestic machines and cut the following steps down to one process. To sew a bound closed seam:

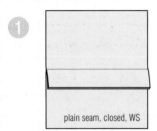

plain seam, closed, WS

Sew a plain seam (see p. 19) and press the seam allowances to one side.

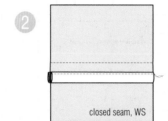

closed seam, WS

Bind using method below.

To sew a bound open seam:

fold
fold
fold

grainline

Take two garment sections with ½in (1.2cm) seam allowances. Cut a bias fabric strip for the binding to the length required and 1½in (4cm) wide; this allows for the strip becoming narrower as it is sewn. Press the binding strip into four equal sections along its length or use a bias-tape maker if available.

RS

Sew the strip onto one of the garment sections right sides together along the pressed crease line.

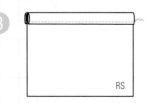

RS

Fold the binding strip onto the wrong side, so that it encloses the raw edge. Press. From the right side, edgestitch the folded edge on the wrong side.

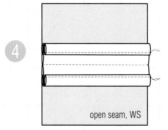

open seam, WS

Repeat for the other side. Sew together the sections as plain seam (see p. 19).

NOTCHES

Notches are clipped markers in the seam allowances of paper pattern pieces. Pattern notchers are used for making them. These notches are transferred onto fabric as a chalk line or a small (⅛in/3mm) snip. Notches can also be made by snipping a small triangle into the edge of the pattern.

Notches denote important positions such as the waistline, hip line, pleats, or darts. They help to indicate match points on complicated seams, such as highly curved seams where the lengths of seam edges of concave and convex curves can differ greatly. As a rule, notches should be placed in the middle of a long section to ensure that garment parts do not stretch while being sewn.

Notches provide essential markers for pattern cutters and machinists. For pattern cutters, they can indicate garment balance. The balance, or pitch points, on sleeves ensure that the sleeve falls correctly and does not twist when inset. For the machinist, notches enable pieces to be matched up accurately, and allow fullness to be allocated precisely in areas with ease.

PIPED SEAM

A piped seam is an ornamental seam, used to enhance style lines. It can be used with many fabrics, but thinner to medium-weight materials are best used for the piping casing, as thicker fabrics may be too bulky. For an alternative look, the cord can be removed once the seam has been stitched. To sew a piped seam:

1

Use a ½in (1.2cm) seam allowance on seam sections. Cut a bias strip of fabric for the binding 1¼in (3cm) wide for the length needed, plus a small amount extra.

2

Fold the bias strips in half, wrong sides together, enclosing a length of cord against the folded edge.

3

With the zipper foot attached, sew a line of stitching close to the piping.

4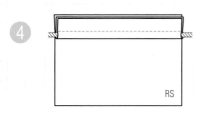

Matching the seam edges, sew the piping right side together to one of the garment sections with the same zipper foot along the same line.

5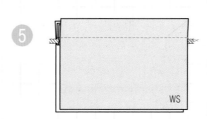

Attach the other garment section as before and press seams outward.

6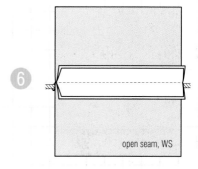

Piped seam from the wrong side.

7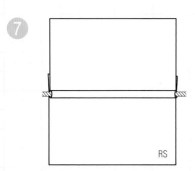

Piped seam from the right side.

THE BASICS
Fundamentals of a garment

DARTS

Darts provide a three-dimensional structure to a garment. They suppress volume that may be required in one section of a garment, but unwanted elsewhere. Traditional areas for dart shaping are the bust, chest, waist, and hips—all areas that contour the natural body shape. However, darts can be applied anywhere in a garment where the design dictates, such as on a sleevehead to provide extra fullness. Darts can be a necessity to provide shape, but this does not mean that they have to be boring or ugly; a well-placed dart can enhance the lines of a design.

In the industry, darts are marked by a drill hole inset to a set distance (i.e., ½in/1.2cm from the apex of the dart and ⅛in/3mm from the width), but tailor's tacks or a chalk mark are equally sufficient.

While stitching a dart, it is possible to back-tack in order to secure the stitch at the apex. However, in certain instances this can be bulky, and creates a bump when pressed. For the following methods of dart construction, backstitching is not used; instead, the hanging threads are tied off at the tip of the dart. This technique is more time-consuming but gives a cleaner finish.

When a dart is pattern-cut, the dart lines are marked with straight lines. However, most darts need to be curved off, or contoured, when stitching, to produce a naturalistic body shape. These curves can be either concave (inward), or convex (outward), depending on the area of shaping.

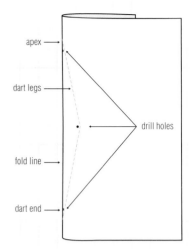

apex

dart legs

drill holes

fold line

dart end

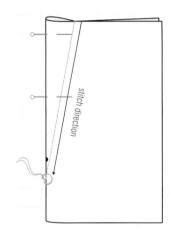

stitch direction

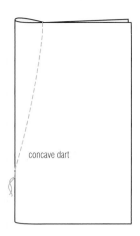

concave dart

BASIC WEDGE DART

To construct a basic wedge dart, fold the dart in half, right sides together, along the fold line up to the apex, matching the notches of the dart at the seam allowances. Stitch along the dart line, dropping down to a smaller stitch length when ½in (1.2cm) from the apex. Without backstitching, sew off the edge of the folded fabric from the apex, leaving threads. Tie off the loose threads into a knot, and trim. Wedge darts can be straight, concave, or convex; we have illustrated a concave dart only.

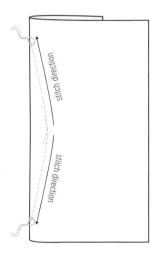

stitch direction

stitch direction

CONTOUR DARTS

Contour or "fisheye" darts are diamond-shaped rather than triangular wedges. They shape the body from bust through waist to hip, but can be used elsewhere. To construct, mark off drill holes at dart apexes and dart widths; fold in half along the fold line, with right sides together. Stitch from the center of the dart to the apexes at either end, knotting threads at both points. To stop the dart from pinching at the center, slightly curve off the angle at the widest part of the dart when stitching.

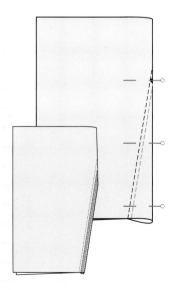

TRIMMING DARTS

Some darts, such as at the waist on a tailored jacket, need to be trimmed back and opened up so they lay flat from the right side. However, there are other instances, such as for sheer fabrics, or with large and bulky darts, where darts are best trimmed down. Here, sew another line of stitching ⅛in (3mm) in from the original stitch line. Overlock off the excess up to this new edge.

CURVED/SHAPED DARTS

To construct curved or shaped darts:

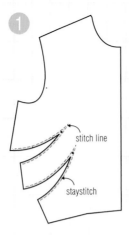

stitch line

staystitch

Prepare by marking off drill holes onto
fabric. To stop the dart from stretching,
staystitch ⅛in (3mm) in from dart
stitch line.

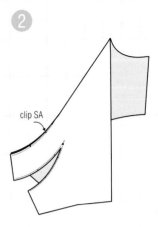

clip SA

Fold through the center line, and
stitch the dart line as for wedge darts.
Clip into the dart to allow it to lay flat
as a curve.

DART TUCKS

Dart tucks are darts that are stitched only partway to the apex, allowing the fullness to be released at
a specific point; once pressed, these may look like an inverted pleat or knife pleat, depending on how
the dart is pressed. For a knife pleat, the dart is pressed cleanly to one side; for an inverted pleat, the
dart amount is pressed flat equally on either side of the stitch line.

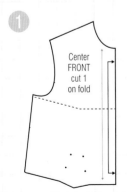

Center
FRONT
cut 1
on fold

Mark drill holes on the pattern just
inside the stitch line to ensure that
marking does not show after the
dart is sewn.

Prepare by marking off drill holes onto
the fabric. Fold fabric along center of
dart and stitch outside drill holes.

inverted
pleat

knife
pleat

Lightly press the finished dart tuck.
Any dart excess can be pressed cleanly
to one side or divided equally either
side of the stitch line.

PRESSING DARTS

Press each dart as soon as it has been constructed. Horizontal darts are generally pressed downward, and vertical darts toward the center front or center back.

REINFORCED DARTS

Reinforced darts can be produced by stitching off from the apex onto a small piece of fabric; this negates the need to backstitch and is more secure than just knotting off the thread ends. This is a common method in tailoring, as it provides a flat appearance, but is also suitable for fine fabrics that are prone to fraying, such as organza, voile, and fine cotton lawns. To construct reinforced darts:

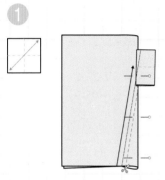

① Bias-cut a small piece of fabric 1½ x 1½in (4 x 4cm). Fuse, if required. Fold in half and place the folded edge at the end of the dart, with the apex of the dart at the center of the piece. Sew the dart as normal, stitching off from the tip onto the reinforcing fabric section. Cut through the folded dart up to the attached fabric.

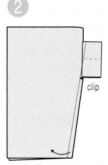

② Clip into the dart at this point so that the dart tip can be pressed to one side.

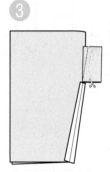

③ Trim around the excess of the reinforcing fabric to the shape of the tip, leaving a rounded amount around the point of the dart.

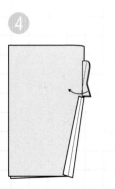

④ Open out the reinforcing section.

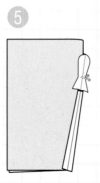

⑤ Snip as shown; this helps keep the tip flat when pressed.

⑥ Press the dart open.

THE BASICS
Fundamentals of a garment

CHAPTER 3: FABRIC CONSIDERATIONS

INTERFACINGS

There are many ways to add body and weight to a material, helping it to hold its shape. Most methods use other fabrics as support. These interfacings can either be sewn in place, for instance as a canvas to support the front of a tailored jacket, or fused onto the wrong side of the fabric.

TYPES OF INTERFACING

A wide array of interfacings are available, each with different properties that are suitable for various fabrics and uses.

- **Woven interfacings:** A wide variety of weights of fabric (usually cotton), with very little give or stretch.
- **Vilene interfacing:** A brand of nonwoven fabric available in a range of thicknesses, and in fusible and stitch-on versions.
- **Reinforced or staystitched interfacings:** These have fine stitch lines running in one or two directions that support in their specified direction. They're often used across a pocket on a jacket to stop it stretching.
- **Stretch fusibles:** Ideal for stretch wovens and jersey fabrics.
- **Leather, suede, and fur interfacings:** These use a glue with a low melting temperature so as not to damage the material.
- **Engineered fusings and front fusibles:** Open knitted interfacings used to add support to suitings while keeping the drape qualities of the fabric.
- **Canvas and horsehair:** Used mainly in tailoring. Made from mixes of wool, linen, hair, and viscose, and available in varying weights. They offer a permanent support to areas on a jacket such as the chest, shoulder, sleevehead, and collar, and are also used in corsetry and underskirts for strength and structure. Fusible canvases can also be found.
- **Crinoline:** Stiff netting used to support voluminous shapes such as full skirts.
- **Wadding/padding:** Can be used to support specific areas or a whole garment in order to change silhouette. Can also be used to add warmth in a garment.

FUSIBLE INTERFACING

Fusible interfacing uses a heat-reactive, meltable glue, which is sprayed thinly and evenly over the interfacing, or "printed" on with glue dots. The fusing is then affixed to the fabric using an iron. Do not use a steam setting as this can prevent the fusing from adhering correctly. It is important that the correct temperature and time of fusing is achieved to prevent delamination, whereby the layers of self and fusing come apart. Over time, with use and washing, this may still happen; certain companies will not use fusibles for this reason.

When using fusibles, care must be taken that the glue does not come through onto the right side of the fabric; this is called strike-through. Strike-back, conversely, is where the glue seeps through to the back of the interfacing. For transparent or very thin fabrics, a layer of organza or organdy of the same color can be sewn in to give "invisible" added structure. Alternatively, an extra middle layer of the self-fabric, such as crepe georgette for a collar, can be used for a softer support; this may be more suited to the desired feel and look of the end garment.

When fusing, sections within the body of the garment traditionally call for a supple, flexible interfacing, whereas areas around the profile edge, such as the collar, rever, hem, and cuff, need stiffer support in order to prevent warping over time. Test the fusing beforehand on your fabric; it should enhance the fabric, without hardening or looking obviously fused.

OTHER FORMS OF SUPPORT

As well as interfacings there are other materials that can be used
to support fabric to create a specific shape or silhouette that would
not be formed naturally.

BONING

Boning was traditionally used in the making of corsetry, whereby reshaped
whalebones were stitched into channels within the garment to attain a desired
body support and silhouette. Today, products such as Rigilene, made of a series
of polyester rods woven together, and plastic boning are available to give the
same effect. Metal boning has the added bonus of being able to curve both
vertically and horizontally, and therefore better contours to the body. This
metal boning can be shortened, but less easily so than Rigilene; metal boning
has rounded ends that protect the wearer, and must be taken off and
reattached to shorten. When shortening Rigilene, it is best to curve off the
cut ends or protect the wearer by stitching over a soft fabric such as velvet.

Boning can either be attached to the wrong side of the self-fabric or lining
for a decorative finish (this will give visible top-stitching), or applied to an
interfacing of canvas or cotton. This interfacing is layered between the self and
the lining, and provides an invisible support. Rigilene can be positioned in place
and stitched through; metal boning must be inserted into a channel sewn into
the garment.

SHOULDER PADS

These come in a wide range of styles and applications, from tailored to raglan.
Pads can be custom made to create a specific shape by layering wadding to
the desired thickness and placing it between two pieces of muslin. Use large
stitches to secure the layers together.

1. A bustier dress. Strapless
garments often include a boned
bodice for additional support.

(Photo credit: Fever)

2. Image key
a) Twill-covered boning
b) Spiral wire (to be cut to size)
c) Spiral wire end caps
d) Synthetic whalebone

(Suppliers: Eastman Staples Limited, Vena Cava
Design, Kleins, MacCulloch & Wallis)

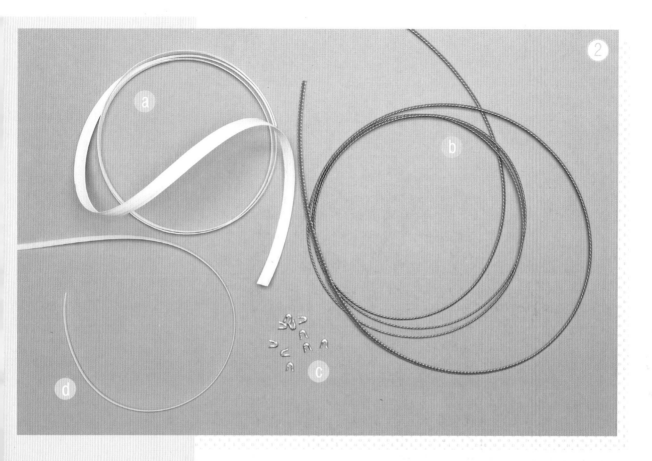

3. Image key
a) Set-in, tailored shoulder pad
(for jackets)
b) Raglan shoulder pad (multiple
use, primarily garments with raglan
or kimono-style sleeves)
c) Women's medium tailored
shoulder pad (for jackets and
soft tailoring)
d) Small fabric-covered foam
shoulder pad (multiple uses:
soft tailoring, tops, and blouses)

(Suppliers: Eastman Staples Limited,
Kleins, MacCulloch & Wallis)

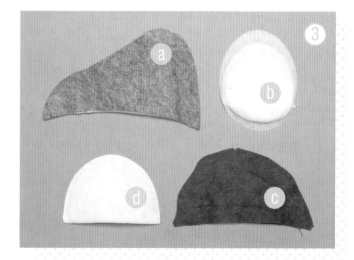

LAYOUT, CUTTING, AND MARKING

Care and attention paid during the layout, cutting, and marking stage of garment manufacture ensures your garment achieves not only the best possible fit and appearance, but also the most economical use of fabric.

GRAIN

The different characteristics of a fabric's grain play an important part in how a garment will look. Incorrect cutting can twist the garment and spoil its appearance; however, once the qualities of grain are understood they can be utilized to great effect.

The grain denotes the direction of threads within a woven fabric. The warp threads, or straight grain, run parallel with the selvage; the weft threads, or crossgrain, run across the fabric, at right angles to the selvage.

The warp threads run continuously down the fabric. They are very stable and provide strength while the fabric is being woven. Weft threads form the weaving pattern and tend to be more elastic than the warp. Even more elastic is the bias of the fabric, which may run at any angle diagonal to the warp and weft. A true bias is at an exact 45-degree angle to the warp and has the greatest amount of give.

Binding strips for seam edges and piping are both cut on this bias line; being bias-cut it easily follows and forms around any curves without distorting the seam. Bias cutting exploits this natural stretch and is often used to create garments that form to the body and fall and drape softly, though this often requires generous amounts of cloth when laying out. Bias cutting lends itself to eveningwear and lingerie.

COMMON GRAINLINES FOR MAIN PATTERN PIECES

Fronts—Parallel to CF.

Backs—Parallel to CB.

Sleeves—On the center line, which can be attained by folding sleeve in half, matching together underarm seams.

Top collars—On CB.

Undercollars—Bias cut or on CB, depending on the look desired. Bias will achieve softer results than a top and undercollar both cut on the CB straight grain.

Lapel facings—Parallel to CF, generally in line with the lapel edge.

Traditional shirt yokes and collars—Crossgrain to utilize warp strength.

Waistbands—Crossgrain to utilize warp strength.

Trouser legs—On the center line, which can be attained by folding the trouser leg in half and matching inside and outer leg seams together.

Patch pockets—Should be derived from the grainline of the piece it is located on. Pay attention to pattern and stripes, as pockets can be cut to either blend into or contrast with the garment section to which they are attached.

1. This striped shirt utilizes panels with contrasting grain direction.

(Photo credit: ASOS)

FABRICS WITHOUT GRAIN

Knitted fabrics such as jersey have no thread direction; however, they must be treated as if they did, using the wales or ribs (lengthwise columns of loops) as the straight grain and courses (knitted rows) as the cross grain.

Felts and some other nonwoven fabrics, such as Tyvek, rubber, and leather, have no grain, and can be cut in any direction. Due to the nature of their construction, these fabrics do not fray in the same manner as wovens.

IDENTIFYING GRAIN

crossgrain (weft)

selvage

selvage

straight grain (warp)

true bias (45°)

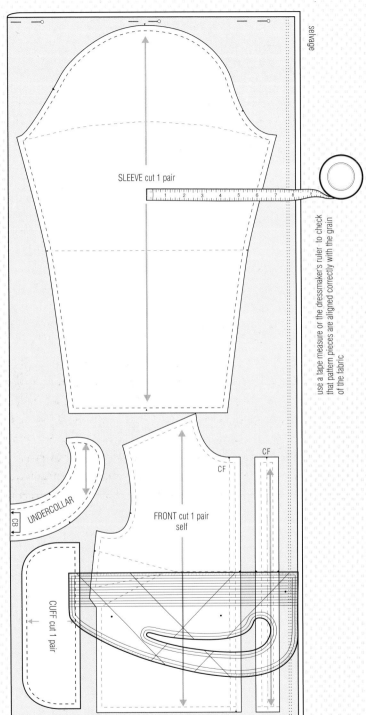

SLEEVE cut 1 pair

use a tape measure or the dressmaker's ruler to check
that pattern pieces are aligned correctly with the grain
of the fabric

UNDERCOLLAR

CB

CF

CF

FRONT cut 1 pair
self

CUFF cut 1 pair

CHECKING AND STRAIGHTENING GRAIN

As fabrics can be distorted out of shape in handling at the textile mill, it is important to check that the warp and weft threads within your fabric are at perfect right angles.

To check the grain, pull on a weft thread at the edge of your fabric length and cut across; if this newly cut edge is not at 90 degrees to the selvage, it will be necessary to straighten the fabric. If marginally off-grain, fold the fabric right sides together, matching and pinning selvage edges every 5in (12.5cm) or so and press; this will realign the weft threads. If the fabric is considerably off-grain, grasp the fabric at the sides and pull across the bias until the right angle between warp and weft is created.

Immersing fabric in warm water beforehand can help to relax fibers; check that the fabric is washable prior to doing so. Fabric that cannot be pulled into shape should be pressed into shape; distortion may not show when the pattern piece is flat but once constructed it will be evident, and impossible to rectify.

PREPARING FABRIC

Depending on the fabric used, you may need to follow certain preparatory methods before it can be cut. Most natural fabrics, apart from silks, will need shrinking, if not already pre-shrunk by the manufacturer. The most common way to do this is to steam press the fabric. Alternatively, you can fold the fabric and immerse it in a basin of hot water for 30–60 minutes. The fabric can then be removed, lightly wrung out, and dried. Laundering or dry cleaning the fabric can also produce the same effect. Synthetic fabrics will not shrink, but pressing without steam will help to remove creases.

Bolts of patterned fabric.

(Photo credit: Ryann Ford)

RIGHT AND WRONG SIDES OF FABRIC

Determining the right and wrong sides of fabric is not always easy, especially if both fabric surfaces are similar. With fabric bought on a roll, the right side typically faces in to protect it from damage. Needle holes on the selvage can also help determine the correct side. On the right side the holes should puncture through, leaving a slightly raised exit on the wrong side. Slubs and imperfections on the wrong side may be evident; the right side may also have a sheen, or particular finish, that differs from the underside. Ultimately, using the right or wrong side is a design choice; your preferred side should be chosen as the "right" side.

PATTERN AND PRINT

When patterning with printed fabric, carefully observe pattern direction and ensure that you lay your pieces onto the fabric for cutting according to its individual properties.

- One-way patterns have a dominant design direction, which means that all pieces must be positioned and cut in the same direction.

- Two-way patterns, such as small ditsy floral prints, have a specific direction, but one that is not so significant as to warrant one-way-only positioning.

- Non-directional patterns, such as polka dots, stripes, or checks, have no specific direction and can be positioned (if the pile allows) in opposite directions.

- Fabrics with border prints, such as for a skirt hem, are often cut on the cross grain so that the border runs horizontally across the garment.

1. Image key
a, b, e, f) Non-directional pattern
c) One-way pattern
d, g) Two-way pattern
Suppliers: Husqvarna Studio (Bath)

PILE DIRECTION

The pile or nap of cloth denotes the direction or lay of the surface fibers on the fabric. These can be divided into two types.

- One-way pile fabrics have a prominent pile that lays in a single direction. Corduroy, suede, fur, and velvet are examples. All pattern pieces must be cut following this direction, which can cause significant fabric waste.

- Two-way pile fabrics have a small pile and allow for positioning sections in opposite directions. This tends to create less waste than one-way pile fabrics.

- Although not technically a napped surface, fabrics such as moiré (watermarked) taffeta or satin reflect light differently depending on the angle; once the desired direction is chosen all pieces must be cut in that direction. This is even more applicable for two-tone fabrics.

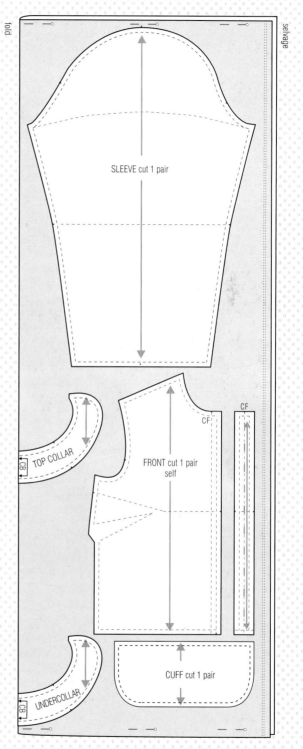

Fabric with a pile or directional print needs to be laid out to ensure all pieces lie in the same direction in the finished garment

THE BASICS
Fabric considerations

SYMMETRY

Most garments have a symmetrical nature, and it is important that stripes, plaids, checks, and prints are cut so that the parts from either side of the garment mirror one another. There are two forms of both: even checks and balanced stripes that repeat symmetrically in either direction, and uneven checks and unbalanced stripes that do not.

Always cut striped or checked pieces individually, marking stripe locations on the edge of the pattern so they can be matched exactly for the opposite, adjoining piece. To achieve a professional look, match horizontal stripes or checked patterns at vertical seams such as the center front and back and side seams. Sleeves should also be cut so that the pattern continues visually at the same height around the garment.

LAYING OUT A PATTERN

The majority of garment pieces are cut on the warp/straight grain; the direction of this grain will be marked clearly on the pattern. To ensure that the grain is precise, each pattern piece should be measured from the selvage to the grainline on the pattern with a ruler or tape, checking at each end of the pattern piece that each is the same distance from the edge. (See diagram on p. 36.)

Care must be taken to cut with the grain as much as possible. Pressing and sewing must also be done with the grain so as not to distort or stretch the fabric. On any bias edges, a line of staystitching $\frac{1}{8}$in (3mm) from the edge will help to stop the piece from stretching, which distorts both length and width. Fusible bias stay tape can also be used for the same result.

THE LAYOUT

In order to produce a garment cost-effectively, pattern pieces must be economically arranged according to grainline, pile direction, and pattern of the fabric. In mass production, this layout is created by patternmaking software so as to limit fabric waste and reduce costs. Most manufacturers aim for at least 80–85 percent efficiency of fabric use. A layout will be made for each fabric used within a garment, including interfacings.

1. A symmetrical print layout is used to great effect in this monochrome waterfall-front cardigan.

(Photo credit: Apricot)

MARKING

Paper patterns can simply be pinned directly to or weighed down (by pattern weights) onto the pressed fabric, and then cut around. Alternatively, a sharp tailor's chalk can be used to mark around the pattern, marking all relevant pointers such as notches, darts, and buttonhole placements.

For finer fabrics, or fabrics on which chalk will not show, tailor tacks or thread marks can be used. These are sewn by hand with a doubled thread and either sewn through once and then loosely knotted or sewn through twice and left. These threads are precise, able to be seen on both sides of fabric, and more permanent than chalk marks; they can be easily removed once their purpose has been served.

On a more industrial scale, drill holes are marked by laser or hole punch to position darts, the marks for which will be set in ¼ in (6mm) from the dart ends. Other marking tools such as air-erasable pens can be used, but need to be tested for suitability on the fabric beforehand.

CUTTING

Most of the hard work in cutting out is in its preparation, ensuring that all pattern pieces have been laid correctly with the grain and marked with all relevant points. From then on, all you need is a sharp pair of shears and a focused eye. However, here are some pointers that can make the process easier.

Use a pair of scissors or shears that feels comfortable in the hand. Large tailor's shears, though weighty, are supported by the table surface; the cutter guides, rather than holds, the shears. Large scissors can be used with as much precision as small ones, if used with care. Separate shears should be kept for paper and fabric; cutting paper dulls the blade, which can damage fabric when cutting.

Do not cut against yourself; position your body into the cut line, and cut with rather than into the grain. Turn sections to make it easier, and always keep sections flat when cutting. Use the point of the scissors to clip into notches.

THE BASICS
Fabric considerations

ORDER OF MAKE

Once you have cut out and fused all the relevant sections, lay out the pieces into the basic shape of the garment to check that you have all parts, and that each piece is cut correctly—that is, the right way up, with the pattern or nap in the same direction, and so on.

To make the construction process swift and efficient, position pieces in the right sequence for manufacture, ordering pattern pieces by size with larger pieces at the bottom, smaller on top, and symmetrical pieces placed right sides together. Keep any trimmings, threads, and buttons with the garment pieces so they are close at hand.

Divide into sections for order of make (see pp. 44–45). Decide whether you need to sew a complicated pocket or put together an intricate section first. Some processes such as plackets, button stands, pockets, and zippers need to be completed or sewn when the piece is flat. Parts such as collars and neck facings should be attached as soon as the fewest necessary seams have been joined, and while the garment is still flat (i.e. side seams not sewn), as it is much easier to handle at this stage.

While sewing, continually check the seam and, if needed, unpick and correct any errors that have occurred. Do not cut corners, as doing so will result in sloppy effects that will undoubtedly show in the final piece. Once a section has been completed, it should be pressed and, if required, neatened and topstitched before moving on to the next step.

Try to simplify handling; control fabric layers by basting them together in stages of two layers at a time—a gathered section onto an interfacing, or layers of frills and flounces. This helps to support each layer; the staystitching acts as seam reinforcement, and the section can be treated as one. Arrange the final closing procedure so as to enhance design; a shirt may be closed by French seaming the underarm/side seam, which is both functional and aesthetic.

Bear in mind that these are only guidelines; a creative and unconventional approach to the order of make is good if it will achieve a better or more appropriate result—idiosyncratic design elements may dictate this.

ARRANGEMENT OF ORDER

Whether on a small or an industrial scale, garment construction can
be simplified by ordering the assembly into separate processes.

ASSEMBLING

Assembling processes include off processes and in processes. Off processes
concern garment parts that may be constructed separately to the main body,
such as cuffs, collars, and belts. In processes are construction processes that
are integral to a piece, and must be done before attaching as part of the
garment, such as darts, plackets, pockets, and zippers.

LINKING

Linking processes involve the joining together of main garment parts, such
as attaching the collar to the body of the garment and insetting sleeves.

CLOSING

Closing processes involve the construction of seams—such as the underarm
seam on a sleeve or the side seams on a skirt or bodice—that transform the
section from flat to three-dimensional or "tubular." Attaching a lining would
also be considered a closing procedure.

FINISHING

Finishing processes consist of in processes and out processes. In processes
are finishings that are made when the garment is still in sections, such as seam
neatening, overlocking, and buttonholes. Out processes are finishings that
can be done only when the garment is complete, such as attaching closures
and hemming.

1. Double-breatsed cape with
decorative top-stitching and
domed buttons.
(Photo credit: French Connection)

2. Crested jacket. An unusual
button stand can provide an
interesting design feature on
a classic garment.
(Photo credit: La Redoute)

THE BASICS
Fabric considerations

ORDER OF MAKE FOR SELECTED GARMENTS

Although every design is individual, with details that are unique to that piece, there are general guidelines that can be followed when planning the order of construction for certain garment types.

SLEEVE INSERTION: TUBULAR METHOD

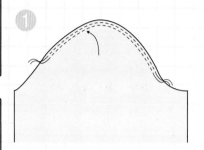

Set machine to largest stitch and sew two rows of machine basting between the notches and within seam allowance (SA).

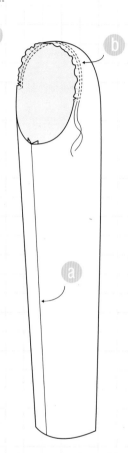

Sew underarm seam, press SA open, and turn to right side (a). Use basting stitch to gauge ease in the crown, ensure fullness is distributed evenly, and note how cap begins to form at shoulder (b).

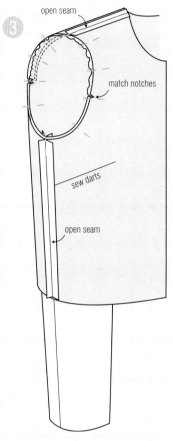

open seam

match notches

sew darts

open seam

Sew darts, side, and shoulder seam, and press SA open. Turn bodice to wrong side and insert tubed sleeve into arm hole. Note sleeve and bodice are placed RS together. Match notches and seams, pinning sleeve at these points first. Place more pins evenly around the sleeve and hand-baste sleeve in place, removing pins as you work. Turn bodice to RS to check fit and balance. Once satisfied with sleeve placement, turn bodice back to WS and machine into position. Ensure all seam allowances are laying flat in correct position as you sew.

BASIC SHIRT

For a basic shirt, sew the body sections first (folding and stitching the button stand before sewing darts). Leave the side seams open. Make up the collar and stand separately and attach. Construct placket on sleeve and attach sleeve to body of shirt (leaving underarm seam open). Sew up the side seam and underarm seam in one go. Attach cuff, buttons, and sew buttonholes. Hem garment.

BASIC SKIRT

For a basic skirt, attach pockets, sew darts and fastenings if necessary, sew body sections of skirt (the main front and back panels), attach waistband, or, if lined, make up complete shell of lining with facings and attach. Hem.

BASIC TROUSER

For a basic trouser, attach pockets and sew fly (attaching front legs). Attach back legs at inside leg seams, then side seams. Afterward, sew up the crotch from front to back. Attach waistband and hem garment.

LINED JACKET

For a lined jacket, first separate outer pieces from facing/lining pieces. Attach pockets and sew darts; depending on the design, you may need to sew darts before pockets. Sew main body of jacket (the main front and back sections), sew side seams and shoulder seams. Construct and attach collar, make sleeves, and inset into arm holes as shown opposite. Make up lining as outer, attaching facings; sew lining to outer, bagging through sleeve. On the lining, open up part of the underarm seam in the sleeve to bag out the cuffs. This opening will be around 4in (10cm), depending on garment size/bulk, though you may need to open up more if it is difficult to pull the garment through. Once cuffs have been bagged/sewn up, sew up the opening.

1. A well-fitting jacket will have a well-made lining.

(Photo credit: Next)

THE BASICS
Fabric considerations

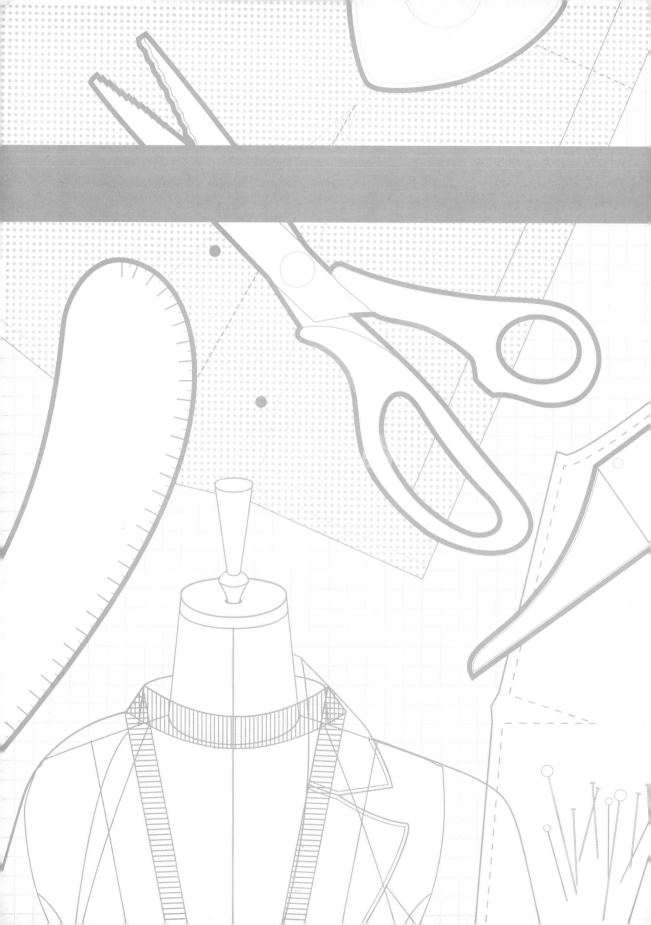

2

DRAFTING TECHNIQUES

CHAPTER 4: DESIGNING PATTERNS FROM SCRATCH

TAKING MEASUREMENTS

Begin by measuring the bust across the fullest part. Allow the tape to rise up 1in (2.5cm) at the center back; if the tape drops, the measurement will decrease and the resulting sloper may be too tight. Compare the measurements you have with those on the chart to find those nearest in bust size and select the appropriate block; if store-bought clothes generally fit well, you may find that the average measurements give successful results. If your measurements differ significantly from those on the chart, it may be necessary to adjust the blocks as per the fitting adjustments in Chapter 5.

NATURAL POSTURE

Ask the person you are measuring to stand naturally, looking forward. If they don't have an upright posture, do not mask their true figure with one. Horizontal measurements can be taken snugly as varying amounts of ease will be added into the sloper.

		SMALL INCHES	SMALL CM	MEDIUM INCHES	MEDIUM CM	LARGE INCHES	LARGE CM	OWN MEASUREMENTS
1	Bust	$32^{1/4}$	82	$34^{5/8}$	88	37	94	
2	Waist	$24^{3/8}$	62	$26^{3/4}$	68	$29^{1/8}$	74	
3	High hip	$29^{1/8}$	74	$31^{1/2}$	80	$33^{7/8}$	86	
4	Hip	$34^{5/8}$	88	37	94	$39^{7/8}$	100	
5	Cross back	$12^{15/16}$	32.9	$13^{1/2}$	34.4	$14^{1/8}$	35.9	
6	Cross front	12	30.6	$12^{3/4}$	32.4	$13^{7/16}$	34.2	
7	Shoulder	$4^{5/8}$	11.8	$4^{3/4}$	12.2	$4^{15/16}$	12.6	
8	Neck size	$13^{15/16}$	35.5	$14^{9/16}$	37	$15^{1/8}$	38.5	
9	Bicep	$10^{5/8}$	27	$11^{1/4}$	28.5	$11^{13/16}$	30	
10	Wrist	6	15.3	$6^{1/4}$	16	$6^{1/2}$	16.7	
11	Nape to waist	$15^{7/8}$	40.4	$16^{1/8}$	41	$16^{3/8}$	41.6	
12	Front shoulder to waist	$15^{7/8}$	40.4	$16^{1/8}$	41	$16^{3/8}$	41.6	
13	Arm hole	8	20.4	$8^{1/4}$	21	$8^{1/2}$	21.6	
14	Sleeve length	$22^{3/4}$	57.8	23	58.5	$23^{1/4}$	59.2	
15	Waist to knee	$22^{3/4}$	57.8	23	58.5	$23^{1/4}$	59.2	
16	Waist to hip	$7^{15/16}$	20.2	$8^{1/8}$	20.6	$8^{1/4}$	21	
17	Waist to floor	$40^{3/8}$	102.5	41	104	$41^{1/2}$	105.5	
18	Body rise	$10^{5/8}$	27	11	28	$11^{3/8}$	29	

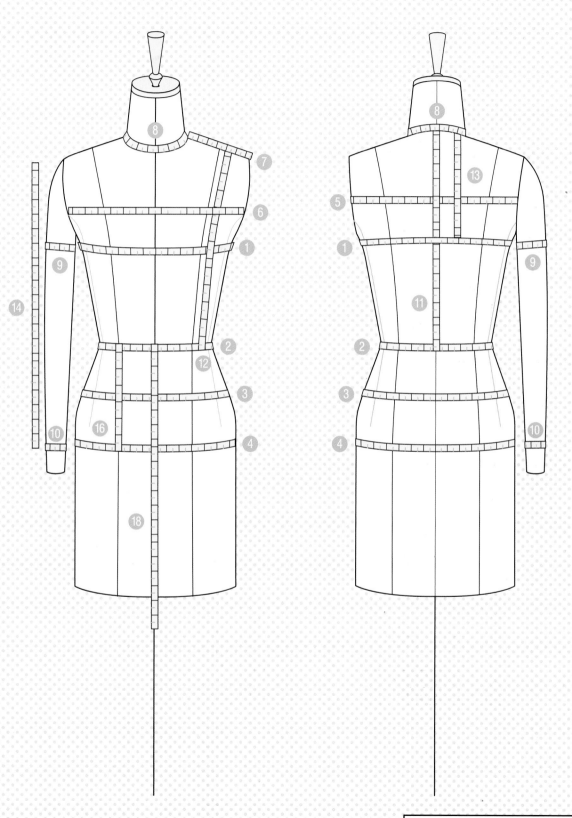

MAKING BASIC SLOPERS

The following basic slopers (templates) form the basis for most of the pattern-drafting techniques in this book. They require scaling to full size, as keyed to the images. After your slopers are scaled, it is essential to construct a muslin (see p. 77) to assess fit and/or any necessary adjustments before committing this template to cardboard: refer to the fitting and alteration exercises in Chapter 5 to tailor your blocks to an individual figure or to correct faults. You may also wish to consider making a direct trace of these blocks to practice the pattern-drafting exercises throughout the book, rather than immediately jumping to full-size experimentation.

(see p. 77)

USING THIS DRESS SLOPER
The basic dress sloper is shown to the hip line and can be extended as required. A copy of this sloper can also be drawn only to the waist, which will prove useful for waisted designs.

SLEEVE BLOCK

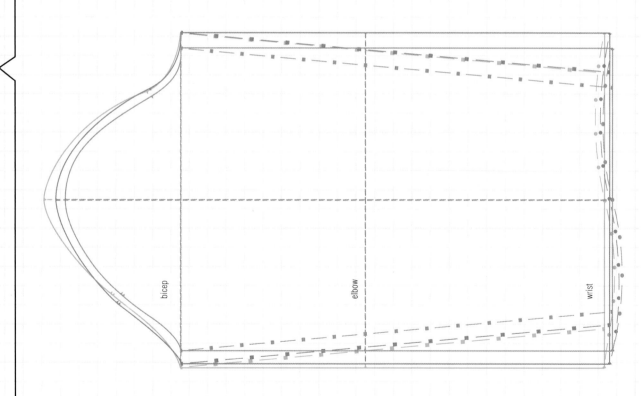

bicep

elbow

wrist

SCALE ▢ =1in (2.5cm)

KEY

 = SMALL   = MEDIUM   = LARGE

`'—•—'` = CLOSE-FITTING

`'—•—'` = SHAPED CUFF

DRESS BLOCK

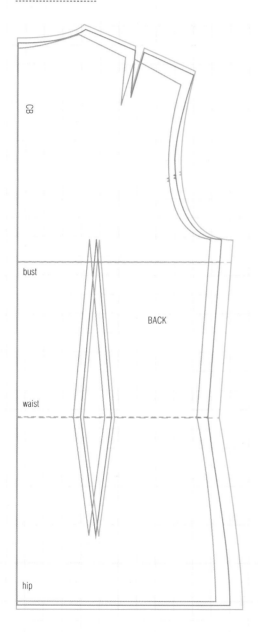

CB

bust

BACK

waist

hip

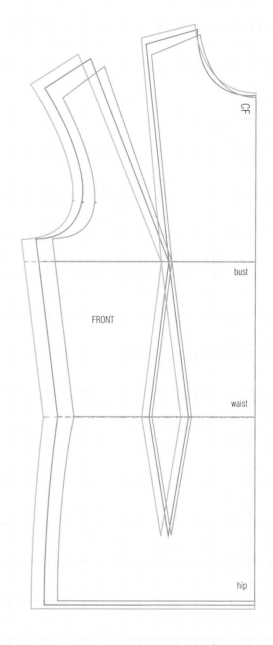

CF

bust

FRONT

waist

hip

SKIRT BLOCK

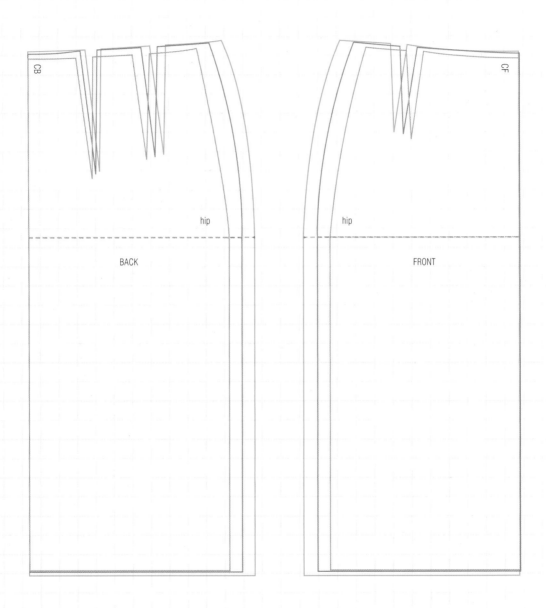

CB

CF

hip

hip

BACK

FRONT

SCALE ▣ = 1in (2.5cm)

1. Charlotte vintage stripe dress.

(Photo credit: Fat Face)

2. Chiffon batwing blouse.

(Photo credit: Blue Inc)

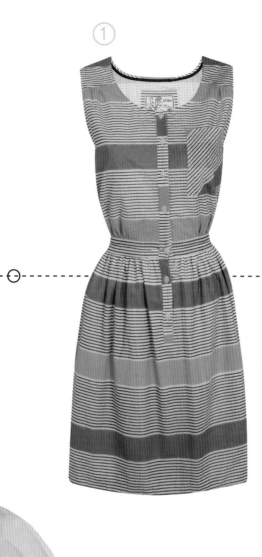

MAKING CULOTTES FROM THE SKIRT SLOPER

A culotte, or divided skirt, is a versatile fashion shape. This type of garment falls flatter from the waistline than a conventional trouser. The basic skirt sloper forms the starting point for this drafting process.

Trace around both front and back basic skirt blocks, ensuring you have enough room on your paper for the crotch extension. Measure the front and back slopers separately along the hip line and make a note of both figures. Once drafted, this sloper can be extended to the desired length and further manipulated as per the skirt. It is readily converted to styles based upon the A-line and panel skirt techniques, or connected to a bodice to create a romper.

①

1. This cotton romper uses a culotte skirt joined to a simple bodice with a gathered waist.

(Photo credit: Apricot)

BASIC SKIRT BLOCK

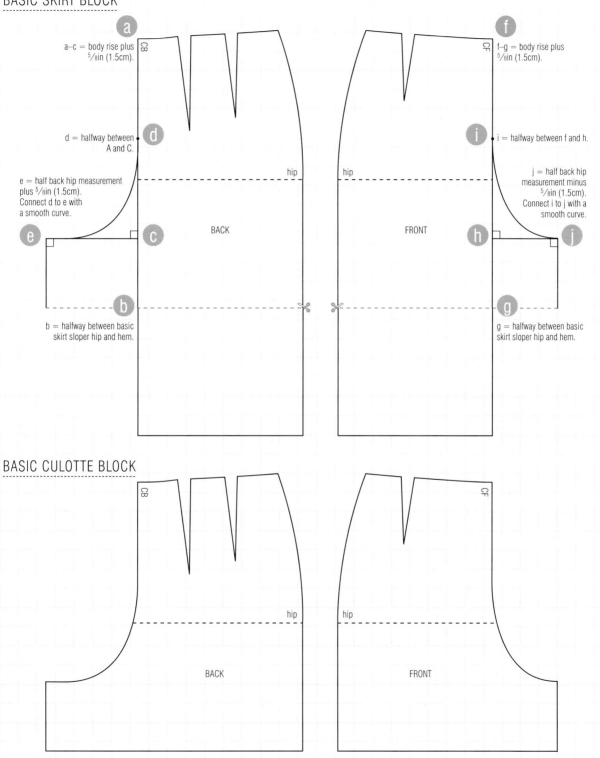

a–c = body rise plus ⁵⁄₈in (1.5cm).

d = halfway between A and C.

e = half back hip measurement plus ⁵⁄₈in (1.5cm). Connect d to e with a smooth curve.

b = halfway between basic skirt sloper hip and hem.

BACK

hip

f–g = body rise plus ⁵⁄₈in (1.5cm).

i = halfway between f and h.

j = half back hip measurement minus ⁵⁄₈in (1.5cm). Connect i to j with a smooth curve.

g = halfway between basic skirt sloper hip and hem.

FRONT

hip

BASIC CULOTTE BLOCK

hip

BACK

hip

FRONT

DRAFTING TECHNIQUES

Designing patterns from scratch

PATTERN DESIGN ESSENTIALS

The following techniques are essential to ensure that your finished garment has the best possible appearance, and should be undertaken after completing the draft pattern.

CHECKING THE RUN OF A PATTERN

Once the pattern-drafting process is complete, you need to ensure that the pattern pieces will work together harmoniously during construction. To check the run of a pattern:

1. Pattern pieces that will be sewn together should be laid next to each other with edges touching: check how they interact and, if necessary, draw a smooth continuous line to bridge seams. This process makes shapes easier to sew together as well as helping to avoid unsightly angles in a finished garment, a fault that can be particularly evident at side seams and on mirrored pieces cut on the fold.

2. Laying pattern pieces together before cutting out also ensures that measurement inconsistencies are noticed and corrected before time and money are wasted with easily avoided mistakes. Small differences in length between pieces can generally be evened out; simply redraw a bridging line using the half/half method: add to the shorter line, remove from the longer.

MEASURE TWICE; SEW ONCE

Always check measurements before committing a pattern to fabric, noting measurements on each pattern piece. Check that notches are correctly positioned, especially after a pattern alteration. Curved pattern pieces should be measured using the tape's edge.

1. A dress featuring asymmetric tuck darting.

(Photo credit: Freemans)

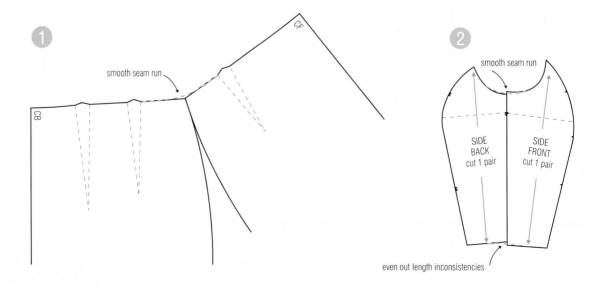

TRUING UP DARTS

This process ensures that the dart excess will maintain the same profile as the seam allowance after construction. To true up darts:

1. Fold pattern paper along dart legs and drop dart into position.
2. Use the tracing wheel to roll through side seam.
3. Note how the waist seam is drawn up at an angle when dart legs are closed. To compensate, fold pattern and create a smooth continuous line. Open out the pattern paper ready to add seam allowances, observing the extended profile of the dart excess between the dart legs.

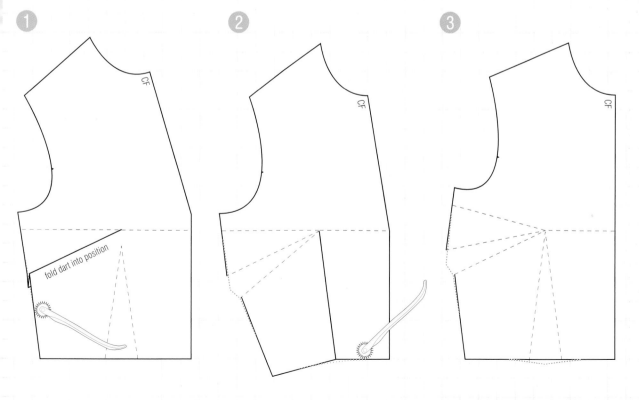

fold dart into position

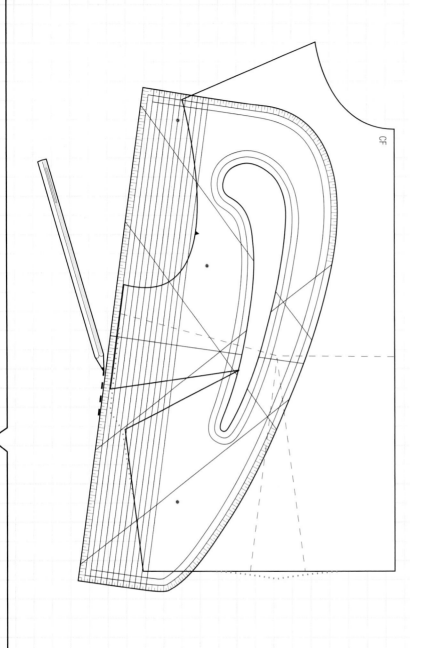

CF

ADDING SEAM ALLOWANCES

Seam allowance (SA) is added after the completion of pattern manipulation, as the blocks used to create individual patterns do not contain the necessary fabric allowance to enable sewing together.

Seam allowance widths vary depending on the required finish: A French seam requires ½in (1.2cm) to accommodate the double turn, whereas a plain seam may only require a ⅜in (1cm) allowance. Curved seams, or seams that will be bagged out, can be trimmed after construction to reduce unnecessary bulk, but you could also draft a narrower seam allowance from the offset.

Many commercial home dressmaker patterns exhibit allowances between ⅝ and ¾in (1.5 and 2cm), building in an extra margin of width that may be needed when the first muslin is fitted. The first working pattern of a style you have drafted from scratch would also benefit from this extra allowance, which can be trimmed from the working pattern should the first fitting muslin prove it unnecessary.

LOWERING THE DART APEX

Lowering the dart apex accommodates the fullness of the bust and avoids a pointed appearance in the final garment. The waist and bust dart apexes are simply shortened by ¾in (2cm) and the dart legs redrawn.

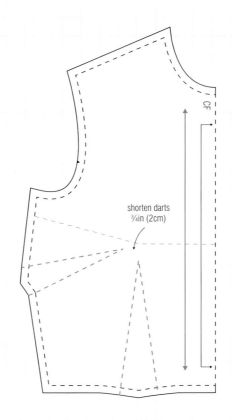

LOW NECKLINES

Any design with a low front or back neckline requires an additional step to remove excess ease through the bust and neckline. This adjustment should also be made to any style with a low rever to ensure the collar does not drag.

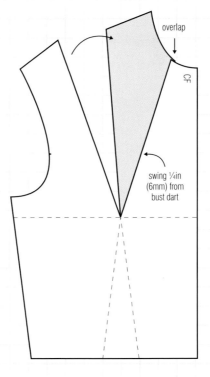

DART MANIPULATION

Dart manipulation is the act of transferring a dart to a new position within a pattern piece, to provide the same amount of suppression and shaping. In the following pages we will explain how to move the darts into standard positions, as well as providing further examples, such as a princess line manipulation, which hides the darts in style lines. Scaled experimentation is to be encouraged, as these positions and techniques covered are by no means exhaustive. The following methods use a basic waisted bodice block with a bust dart.

MOVING DARTS

Darts can be moved horizontally, although there are limits to this. As a general rule, darts can be moved ¾in (2cm) horizontally in either direction with very little trouble, but any more than this and the garment will begin to take on a flatter appearance and start to crease or pull at the side seams. Suppression should be spread evenly around a garment, so that a fully three-dimensional garment is achieved.

STANDARD DART POSITIONS

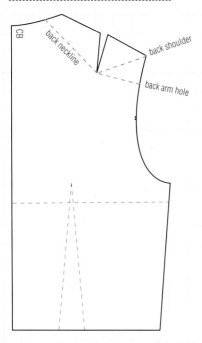

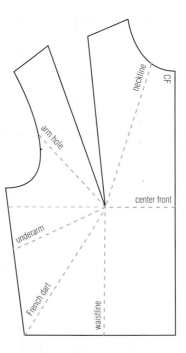

UNDERARM DART

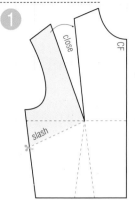

① Mark new dart position and cut along this line.

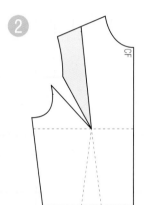

② Pivot the released (gray) section to close the original bust dart position.

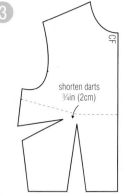

③ Shorten dart apex.

SHOULDER TO ARM HOLE

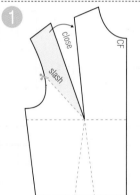

① Mark new dart position and cut along this line.

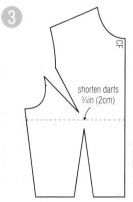

② Pivot the released (gray) section to close the original bust dart position.

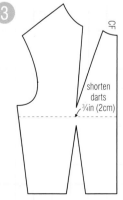

③ Shorten dart apex.

SHOULDER TO NECKLINE

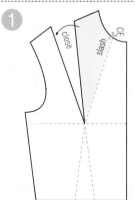

① Mark new dart position and cut along this line.

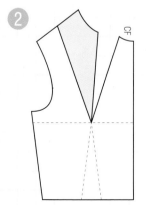

② Pivot the released (gray) section to close the original bust dart position.

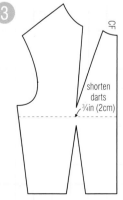

③ Shorten dart apex.

DRAFTING TECHNIQUES
Designing patterns from scratch

SHOULDER TO CENTER FRONT

1 Mark new dart position and cut along this line.

2 Pivot the released (gray) section to close the original bust dart position.

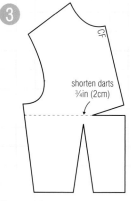

3 Shorten dart apex.

FRENCH DART

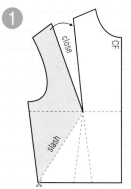

1 Mark new dart position and cut along this line.

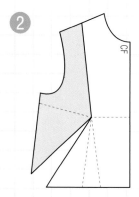

2 Pivot the released (gray) section to close original bust dart position.

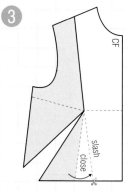

3 Cut along one of the waist dart legs.

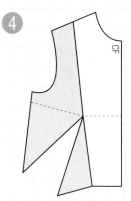

4 Pivot the released (gray) section to close original waist dart position: dart excess from waist and bust dart are now contained in a single dart.

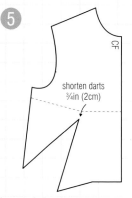

5 Lower dart apex.

BACK SHOULDER DART TO ARM HOLE

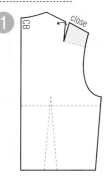

Mark new shoulder dart position and cut along this line; pivot the released (gray) section to close the original shoulder dart position. It is not necessary to shorten the dart apex on a shoulder dart.

BACK SHOULDER TO NECKLINE

Mark new shoulder dart position and cut along this line; pivot the released (gray) section to close the original shoulder dart position. It is not necessary to shorten the dart apex on a shoulder dart.

SHOULDER POINT

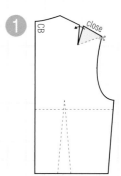

Mark new shoulder dart position and cut along this line; pivot the released (gray) section to close the original shoulder dart position. It is not necessary to shorten the dart apex on a shoulder dart.

SPLIT DART: SHOULDER DART INTO FOUR DARTS

Mark new dart positions and cut along these lines.

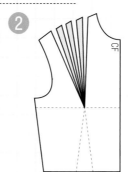

Fan out the released (gray) sections.

Shorten dart apex. Sewing radiating darts can prove tricky on some fabrics: consider using them in combination with dart tucks (see p. 28), as shown here.

SPLIT DART: SHOULDER AND WAIST DART INTO THREE DARTS AT WAIST

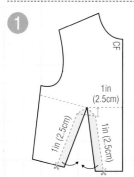

Move bust dart into waist dart. Draw 1in (2.5cm) from dart leg.

Fan out the released (gray) sections.

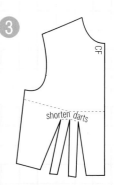

Lower dart apex.

DRAFTING TECHNIQUES
Designing patterns from scratch

CURVED DART

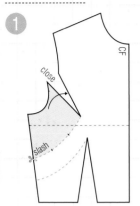

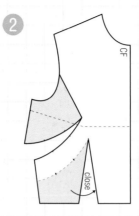

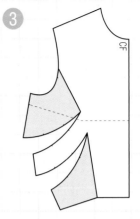

Mark new curved dart positions and cut uppermost line.

Pivot the released (gray) section to close the bust dart. Repeat for waist dart.

Darts in new position. Remember to lower the dart apex.

ASYMMETRIC DART

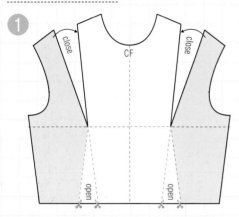

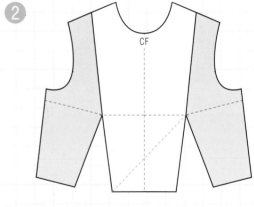

Cut along both waist darts to close the bust dart.

Draw in new dart position.

Cut along this line and close one waist dart.

The dart apex now needs to be lowered as for previous manipulation.

STYLE LINES EXPLAINED

Both a princess line and a Vienna line create shaping by transferring dart excess into seamed style lines. In the case of a princess line, the bust dart is transferred into the shoulder line; with a Vienna line, it is moved to the arm hole.

STYLE LINES

Style lines are seam lines that utilize dart shaping. Within reason, these can be any shape and design. If the chosen seam intersects where the original dart is positioned, the dart can be easily transferred into the seam using the slash and spread method, as shown in diagram 1. If your style line is farther away from the dart, an amount of excess from the remainder of the dart will have to be eased in, or a small dart can be created on the center front panel . In this instance, the style line is marked and the waist darts are redrawn in line with the new panel, using as much or as little of the waist shaping as the design dictates (2). The panels are then separated (3) and a seam allowance added (4).

VIENNA LINE FRONT

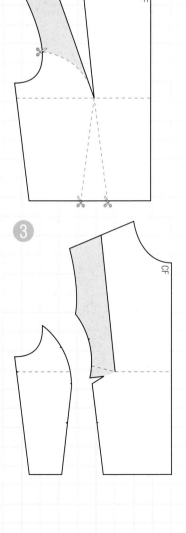
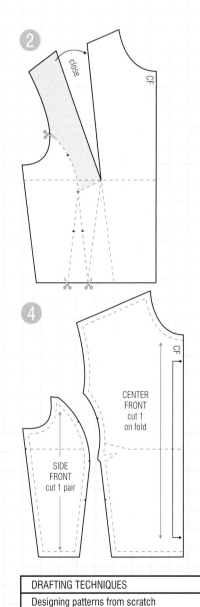

VIENNA LINE BACK

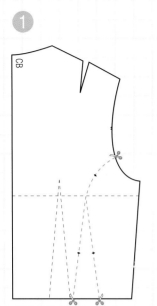

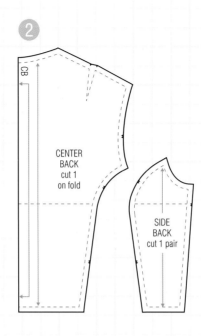

CENTER
BACK
cut 1
on fold

SIDE
BACK
cut 1 pair

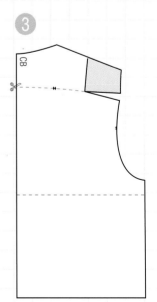

1

1. Color-panel dress with Vienna-line shaping.

(Photo credit: Heatons)

SHOULDER DART INTO BACK YOKE SEAM

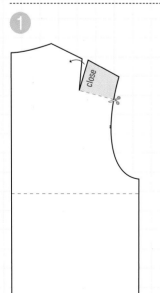

close

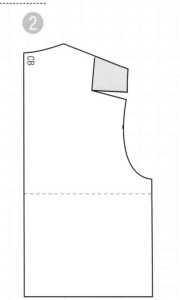

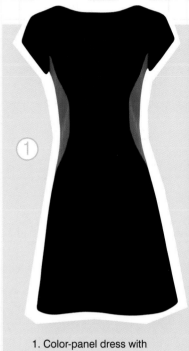

PRINCESS LINE FRONT

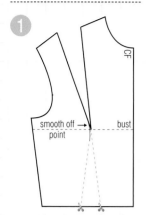

smooth off → point

bust

CF

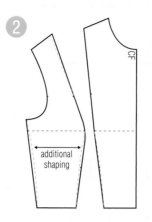

CF

additional shaping

Additional shaping for a closer fit can also be drafted at this stage.

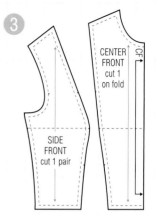

SIDE FRONT cut 1 pair

CENTER FRONT cut 1 on fold

CF

PRINCESS LINE BACK

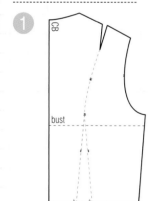

CB

bust

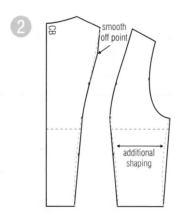

CB

smooth off point

additional shaping

Additional shaping for a closer fit can also be drafted at this stage.

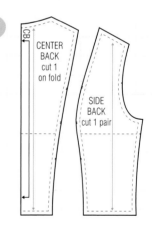

CB

CENTER BACK cut 1 on fold

SIDE BACK cut 1 pair

DRAFTING TECHNIQUES

Designing patterns from scratch

COMBINING AND DIVIDING

Where design dictates, garment sections can be combined, removing seams
that would otherwise distract from the overall look. As a general rule, pattern
pieces with straight edges can simply be joined, while for those with shaping,
any suppression needs to be transferred to another part of the garment.

SHIRT YOKE

This technique is commonly used on traditional shirt yokes and uses both
combining and dividing techniques. It is a development of the back yoke seam
dart manipulation technique covered on p. 66.

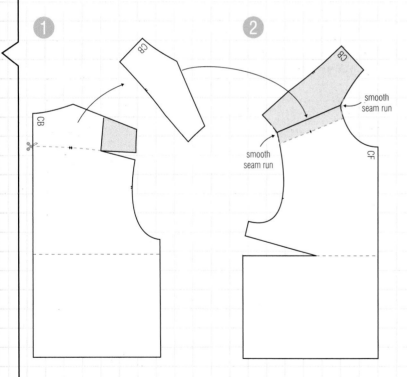

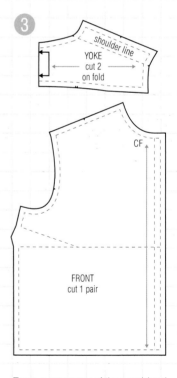

Pivot shoulder dart into the arm hole
and connect point of dart to the CB
with a dashed line. Cut along this line
to release the back shoulder section.

Lay the released back shoulder section
to the shoulder line of the front pattern
piece, touching at the shoulder point
(SP) and shoulder neck point (SNP).

Trace a new copy of the combined
yoke, smoothing the seam runs at neck
and shoulder to give a smooth continuous
line. Add SA and pattern annotation.

DECORATIVE YOKE

In this technique, a more stylized yoke shape is created using the same principles described previously. A section of both the front and back pattern is removed and joined at the shoulder seam.

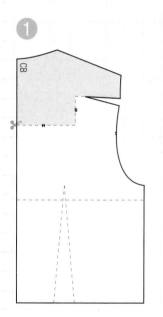

1. A sleeveless shirt with a decorative yoke.

(Photo credit: ASOS)

1

Pivot shoulder dart into the arm hole and connect point of dart to the CB with a dashed line. Cut along this line to release the back shoulder section.

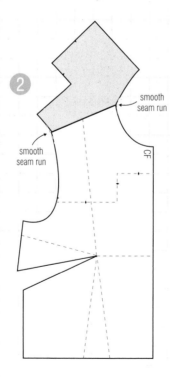

2

Lay the released back shoulder section to the shoulder line of the front pattern piece, touching at SP and SNP.

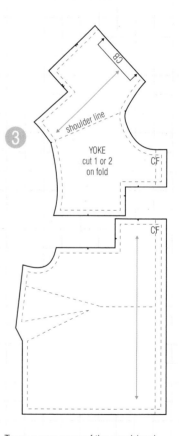

3

Trace a new copy of the combined yoke, smoothing the seam runs at neck and shoulder to give a smooth continuous line. Add SA and pattern annotation.

DRAFTING TECHNIQUES
Designing patterns from scratch

EMPIRE LINE

An empire-line manipulation can provide an excellent basis for a variety of styles. The dart excess in both bodice and skirt sections can be further manipulated—consider using gathers, pleats, and tucks to constrain the fullness contained in the dart. The released lower section can be discarded altogether and a circular or semicircular skirt shape can be drafted or draped to fit the bodice seam.

1. An embellished one-shouldered dress with gathered bodice and empire line.

(Photo credit: Freemans)

2. This paneled skirt has been given additional fullness with godet insertions between seams.

(Photo credit: Mint Velvet)

DRESS BLOCK

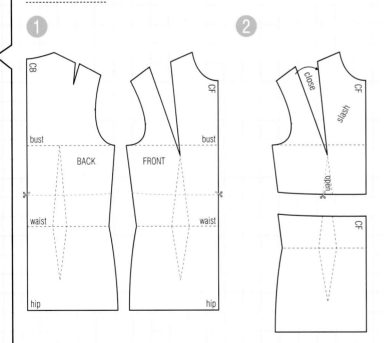

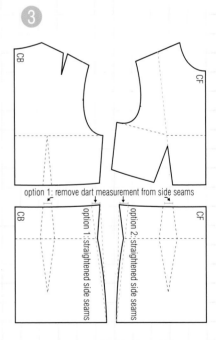

option 1: remove dart measurement from side seams

1 Divide the sloper at the desired height—note that the dividing line is squared off from the center line and gently curved at the side seam.

2 Pivot the bust dart into the desired position.

3 The side seam can be straightened and the dart width can be trimmed from the side seam, as shown in option 1, or the side seam and dart shaping can be maintained for a more fitted style.

PANELED SKIRT

A paneled skirt can be used in conjunction with many other design features: consider the use of pleats, piping, or contrasting fabrics. Alternating the grain direction, on a striped or patterned fabric, can be used to great effect with this simple skirt shape.

① ②

SKIRT BLOCK

① ②

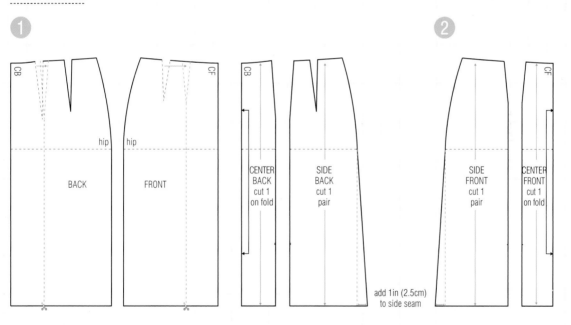

CB

hip | hip

BACK

FRONT

CF

CB

CENTER BACK
cut 1
on fold

SIDE BACK
cut 1
pair

add 1in (2.5cm)
to side seam

SIDE FRONT
cut 1
pair

CENTER FRONT
cut 1
on fold

CF

Starting with the basic skirt muslin, measure the hip line and divide by three. Using this figure as a guide, square a vertical line from the waist to hem at both the CF and CB to create your new seam.

Move the front dart and one of the back darts in line with this newly created seam.

Cut along the style lines to separate your skirt into individual pieces and add 1in (2.5cm) to the side seams to give the skirt a gentle flare from the hips. Add seam allowances and pattern annotation.

DRAFTING TECHNIQUES
Designing patterns from scratch

CREATING YOUR OWN PATTERN BLOCKS

Creating your own customized pattern blocks is well worth the effort.
Once you have taken the time to create your basic patterns, you can use
them to make anything.

CIRCLE SKIRT

Many pattern pieces use circles as a base for their construction. Varying the
grain on circular pieces can give very different results in the finished garment,
depending on fabric choice: experimentation is recommended. To construct
a circle, the radius must be known. To find it use the calculation:

radius = circumference ÷ 6.28.

The waistline measurement gives you the inner circumference required.
For a skirt with a waist measurement of 26¾in (68cm), the inner radius
will be 4¼in (10.8cm):

26¾in (68cm) ÷ 6.28 = 4¼in (10.8cm)

CALCULATING RADIUS

The circumference of a circle
is the measurement around a circle;
the radius is a line from the center
of the circle to its outer edge.
Radius = circumference ÷ 6.28.

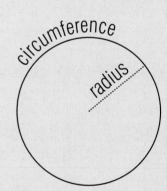

1. Leather circle skirt from
Principles by Ben de Lisi.

(Photo credit: Debenhams)

CIRCLE SKIRT

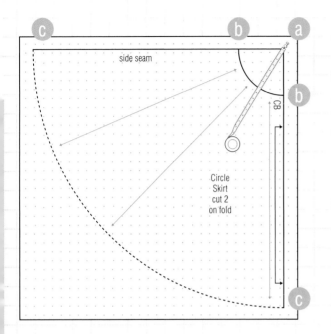

To draft a circular skirt, first calculate the radius (radius = a–b), then square off from point a. Next, draw a quarter circle to connect both points b and then draw another quarter circle from c–c: Desired skirt length = b–c.

SEMICIRCLE SKIRT

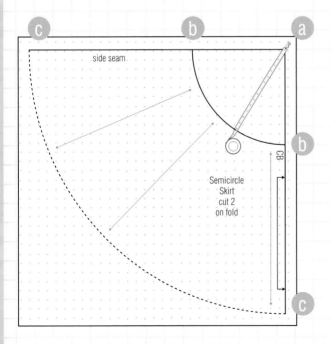

To draft a semicircular skirt, first calculate the radius (twice radius = a–b), then square off from point a. Next, draw a quarter circle to connect both points b and then draw another quarter circle from c–c: Desired skirt length = b–c.

DRAFTING TECHNIQUES
Designing patterns from scratch

A-LINE SKIRT

1

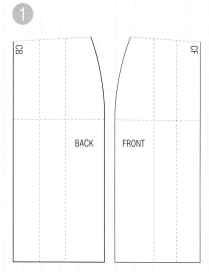

Draw a straight line connecting the waist at center back and side seams. Divide this line by three and square a line from waist to hem to create panel seams. Repeat for front.

2

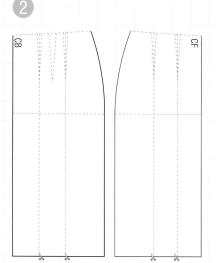

Back: create two ⅜in x 5¼in (1cm x 13.5cm) darts on the panel seam lines. Create another dart in the center of these new darts measuring ¾in x 5¼in (2cm x 13.5cm). Front: create two ⅜in x 4in (1cm x 10cm) darts on the panel seam lines.

3

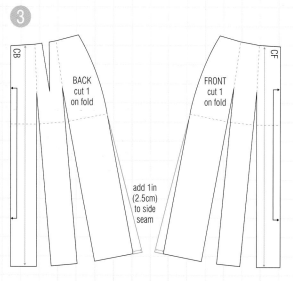

Back: slash and spread both ⅜in (1cm) darts to add volume at hem. Add 1in (2.5cm) to side seam. Repeat for front.

1. A-line skirt with scalloped layer detailing.

(Photo credit: Fever)

EASY-FIT GARMENT OR OVER-GARMENT

The basic dress sloper can be converted into an easy-fitting sloper to create garments with a more relaxed fit or as a basis for over-garments. This sloper can also provide an excellent basis for jersey or knitwear garments. The basic block exhibits no suppression of fullness at the waist or shaping at the side seam; this can be added as your design dictates.

EASY-FIT BODY

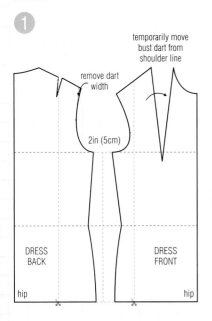

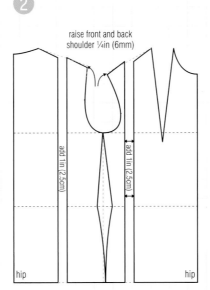

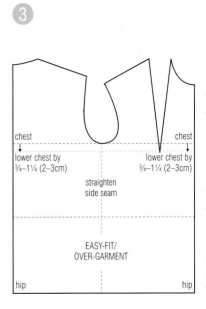

Trace around front and back slopers, leaving a gap of 2in (5cm) between side seams. Temporarily pivot bust dart from shoulder line and remove back shoulder dart width from back arm hole. Squaring off from bustline, draw a dashed line vertically through front and back blocks into the center of the shoulder line.

Raise front and back shoulder line ¼in (6mm). Slash along vertical line, opening out front and back slopers 1in (2.5cm) until side seams touch.

Lower chest line ¾–1¼in (2–3cm) on both front and back slopers and straighten side seam.

EASY-FIT SLEEVE

1

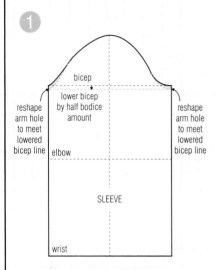

Lower bicep line by half the amount the chest line was lowered in the previous step. Reshape arm hole to meet lowered bicep line.

2

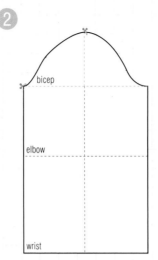

Slash crown horizontally along new bicep line and then vertically through the center line.

3

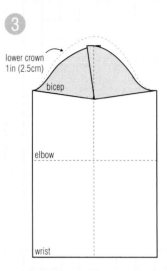

Pivot the two released crown sections downward, lowering the crown by the same amount added through the front and back bodice. Redraw crown with a smooth continuous line.

4

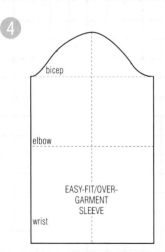

Trace manipulated sleeve, creating a smooth continuous line at crown. Create a fitting muslin to check adjustments; only once you are happy with the fit of your sloper should the block be committed to cardboard.

MUSLINS

A muslin or *toile* (derived from the French term for cloth, namely canvas), is essentially a garment prototype; "toile" can also be the fabric used in its creation. Up to this point, the initial pattern draft is just a hypothesis in pattern cutting, and is only proven when the muslin is created and then tested on the fitting model or dress form. In the transformation from a flat to a three-dimensional shape, many unforeseen problems can arise; the muslin is a means of testing the design so that these may be corrected and the pattern resolved. It is a chance to see proportion, silhouette, style lines, and design details. For these reasons, lighter-colored fabrics are employed, as these best serve to highlight distortions in the fit of the muslin.

Due to the nature of the muslin process, the muslin is often produced in calico, an inexpensive, unbleached cotton fabric, available in many qualities from muslin to heavy canvas-like weights. Primarily, the muslin must be made in a fabric that behaves most similarly to the one that will eventually be used, so that the effects of weight, drape, stretch, and other properties are taken into account. The muslin should include any fastenings, interfacings, interlinings, or understructure that would be integral to the final piece, but would not necessarily be lined or have functional pockets.

The muslin should be constructed with a larger stitch length so that alterations can easily be made. Once proportion and fit have been assessed and corrected, decorative elements, such as pockets and embroidery, can be positioned.

1. Leather-trim
double-breasted coat.
(Photo credit: Mint Velvet)

2. Women's jacket muslin
in medium-weight calico.
(Supplier: Bath Spa University)

3. Paneled culotte muslin
in medium-weight calico.
(Supplier: House of Jo)

DRAFTING TECHNIQUES
Designing patterns from scratch

CHAPTER 5:
FITTING PRINCIPLES AND PATTERN ADJUSTMENTS

After scaling up your blocks, the next step is to measure the block in the same positions where you have taken your measurements—bust, waist, hip, cross shoulder, and so on—and compare the sloper to your own measurements.
It is important that you select the correct sloper to fit your bust and, with the following fitting techniques, tailor your block to fit an individual figure. It is advisable to copy your first block onto paper and only commit it to cardboard after you have made a bespoke block that truly fits your intended figure.

BASIC LENGTH ADJUSTMENTS

Adjustments to the length of the block can be performed by extending or overlapping across the entire width, as shown in the diagrams. The bodice block is shown with adjustments both above and below the waist, but after comparing your measurements to the block you may find only one of these adjustments is necessary, i.e., above or below the waist.

SLEEVE

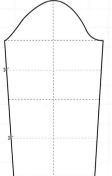

Pattern adjustment
position

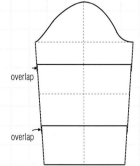

overlap

overlap

Shorten

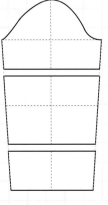

Lengthen

INITIAL ADJUSTMENTS

The blocks contain 1½in (4cm) of wearing ease across the bust, and it is advisable not to "overfit" at this stage. Initial adjustments such as length and width can be made to your block before cutting out your fitting muslin; other alterations may only become apparent when the garment is tried on for the first time. This first fitting muslin should be placed on the figure or mannequin with the right side toward the body and the seam allowances facing outward to allow easy access to unpick and re-pin seams in line with the alterations opposite. After any alteration is made to the sloper, seams should be measured or walked against each other to ensure compatibility.

SKIRT

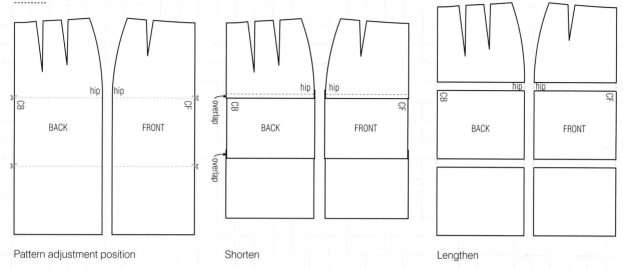

Pattern adjustment position

Shorten

Lengthen

BODICE

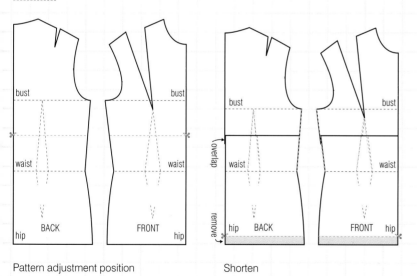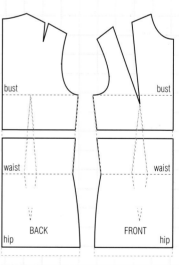

Pattern adjustment position

Shorten

Lengthen

DRAFTING TECHNIQUES
Fitting principles and pattern adjustments

BASIC WIDTH ADJUSTMENTS

If width alterations are being made to an existing style or pattern, the
necessary width should be divided equally between all panels in the design.
For specific adjustments to a dress, skirt, or sleeve, follow the advice below.

BODICE

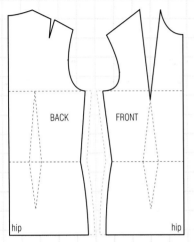

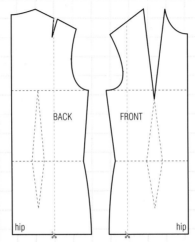

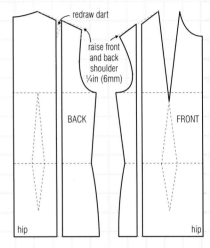

A basic width adjustment of 1in (2.5cm)
or less can be made to your sloper side
seams. If the adjustment is only required
to ensure a good fit at waist or hip, only
add to these sections on your sloper.

Note the scissor icons, indicating
the position for pattern adjustment.

Don't add width through the neckline
or arm hole: this will affect the fit of your
sloper. Divide width adjustment between
front and back slopers and add through
the shoulder in the case of the bodice.

SKIRT

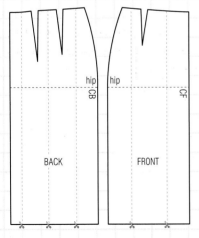

SLEEVE

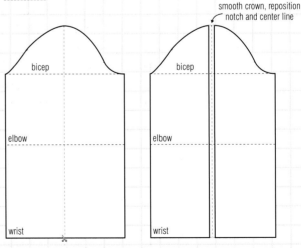

Divide the necessary width adjustment
between the front and back slopers and
add between the darts in the skirt sloper.

The sleeve sloper is divided at the center
line to add or remove width and the
crown is redrawn.

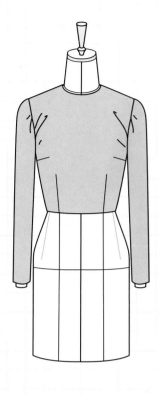

FITTING THE SHOULDERS

The following adaptations will ensure that your sloper sits correctly, hanging smoothly at the shoulder.

SLOPING SHOULDERS

Sloping shoulders cause the bodice and sleeve to crease unattractively at the arm hole. In an over-garment or jacket, this excess may be relieved with a shoulder pad.

To correct: On both front and back pattern pieces, remove excess from the shoulder point, running to zero at the neckline. The underarm will also need to be lowered.

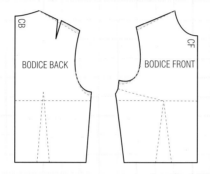

SQUARE SHOULDERS

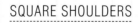

Wrinkles will form across the shoulders and arm hole as the muslin is distorted to accommodate the breadth of the shoulders.

To correct: Slash your paper pattern as directed in the diagram and pivot the shoulder line to create more room for the shoulders. The underarm seam will also need to be raised and, as with any sleeve alteration, it will be necessary to measure the arm hole to ensure compatibility with the sleeve: adjust if required.

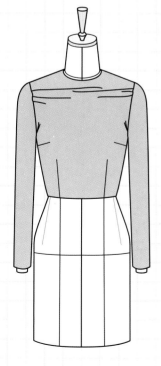

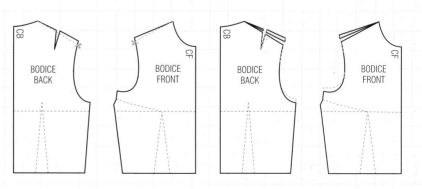

DRAFTING TECHNIQUES
Fitting principles and pattern adjustments

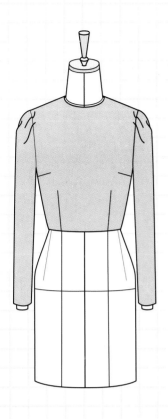

NARROW SHOULDERS

The shoulders and the crown of the sleeve will drop unsupported over narrow shoulders.

To correct: Slash the pattern as shown in the diagram, and pivot the released section to remove width from the shoulder. Redraw the shoulder line.

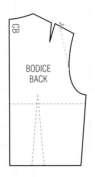

BODICE BACK

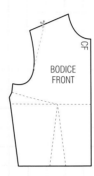

BODICE FRONT

BODICE BACK

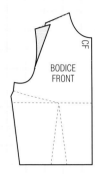

BODICE FRONT

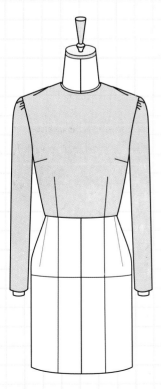

BROAD SHOULDERS

Wrinkles at the crown and shoulder indicate that the fitting muslin does not contain enough breadth for broad shoulders.

To correct: Slash the pattern as shown in the diagram, and pivot the released section to give additional fullness over the shoulder line. Redraw the shoulder line.

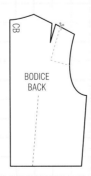

BODICE BACK

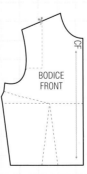

BODICE FRONT

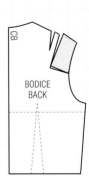

BODICE BACK

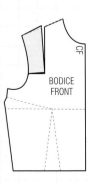

BODICE FRONT

FITTING SLEEVELESS STYLES

Styles without a sleeve may require some adaptation to give a perfect fit.

TIGHT ARM HOLES

The arm hole pulls tight and feels uncomfortable to the wearer.

To correct: Redraw the arm hole to suit the individual figure, ensuring you lower the front and back by the same measurement and check the seam runs interact in a smooth manner.

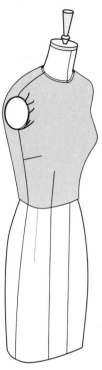

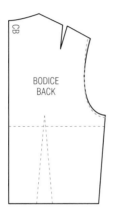
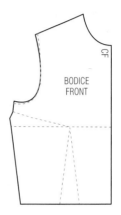

LARGE ARM HOLES

The arm hole is too big, exposing too much of the underarm and/or undergarments.

To correct: Redraw the arm hole, raising the front and back side seams by an equal amount.

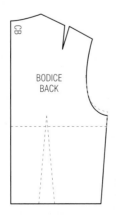
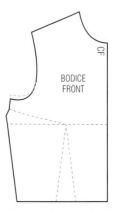

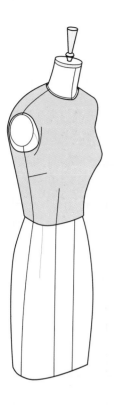

GAPING ARM HOLES

An arm hole that gapes can be indicative of other faults within a muslin: the bust could be too small or the back too large, causing excess fabric to form at the arm hole. If your muslin is gaping at the back arm hole, refer to the alteration advice given for a wide back on p. 92 or a rounded back on p. 91. If the muslin gapes at the front arm hole, follow the instructions for altering the bodice for a large bust on p. 90.

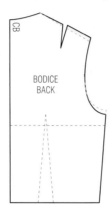

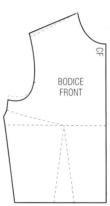

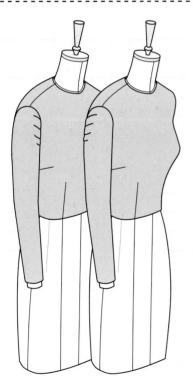

FITTING THE SLEEVES

Sleeves that are poorly fitting not only spoil the appearance of a garment but will be uncomfortable to the wearer.

INCORRECT EASE

Diagonal folds at either the front or back arm hole denote incorrectly distributed ease. This common fault is usually an error created during the construction phase, as ease is not correctly distributed during machining, and is not generally caused by a problem in the pattern or the block.

To correct: Unpick the sleeve and smooth the excess ease either to the front or back of the sleevehead as required. If wrinkles are still apparent, you may need to remove some of the ease from the sleevehead.

NOT ENOUGH CROWN HEIGHT

A sleeve without enough height in its crown will collapse, causing wrinkles to form as it drags across the upper arm.

To correct: Cut the crown along its top third and spread the pattern apart to add the required amount of fullness. Redraw the cap, marking a smooth line to connect the widened pattern pieces.

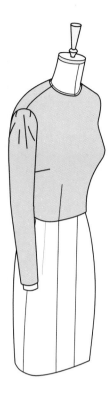

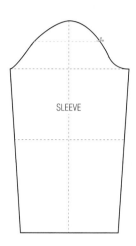

SLEEVE

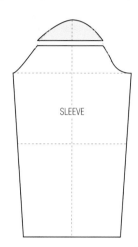

SLEEVE

TOO MUCH CROWN HEIGHT

This problem will cause a furrow to appear below the cap of the sleeve.

To correct: Cut the crown along its top third, as for "not enough crown height." The cap should be overlapped to remove excess height. Redraw a smooth line at the crown and reposition the balance points if necessary.

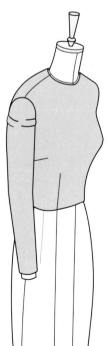

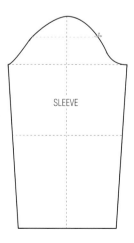

SLEEVE

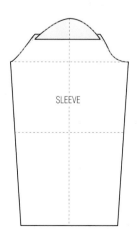

SLEEVE

DRAFTING TECHNIQUES

Fitting principles and pattern adjustments

LARGE ARM

An arm that is too large will cause your muslin to pull and will feel uncomfortable to wear along most of its length.

To correct: Slash and spread both the front and back of the sleeve to add more width throughout the length of the sleeve. If this alteration does not give sufficient room for the ball of the shoulder, it may be necessary to add more height to the crown of the sleeve. The bodice will also need extra room in the arm hole; pivot the released sections and redraw the arm hole and dart.

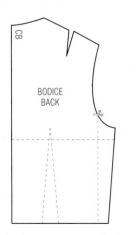

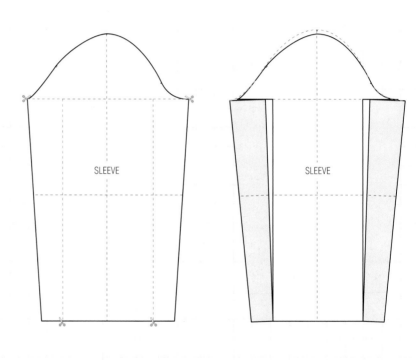

SLEEVE

SLEEVE

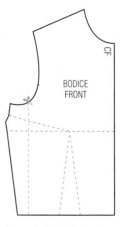

BODICE BACK

CB

BODICE FRONT

CF

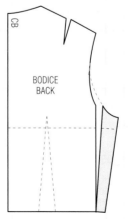

BODICE BACK

CB

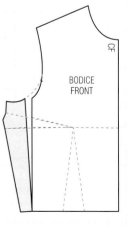

BODICE FRONT

CF

TOO MUCH EASE

Excess ease in a sleeve will create much consternation during construction, causing unwanted wrinkles and gathering around the sleeve cap.

To correct: Cut the sleeve horizontally along the bicep line, and separate the cap vertically into two pieces. Pivot these two pieces downward at the center as shown in the illustration. Redraw the cap with a smooth clean line.

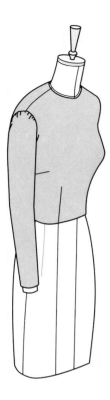

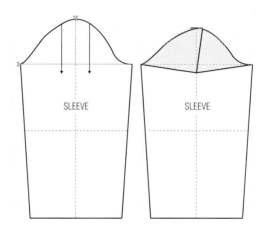

THIN ARM

Excess fabric will sag and wrinkle as it drops over too narrow an arm.

To correct: Cut the sleeve along its whole length and overlap to the desired amount. Raise the arm hole on both the front and back blocks.

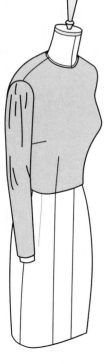

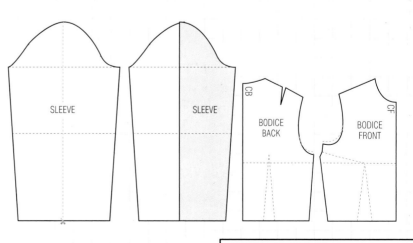

DRAFTING TECHNIQUES
Fitting principles and pattern adjustments

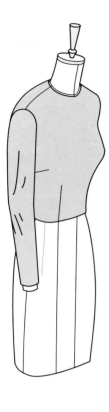

THICK ELBOW

A wide elbow will cause the sleeve to pull from the shoulder, dragging to fit the breadth of the elbow.

To correct: Cut the sleeve along its center up to the elbow line. Pivot the released section to increase the width of the sleeve above the elbow and redraw the back seam and wrist line.

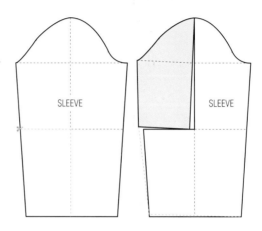

LARGE UPPER ARM

A large upper arm will cause wrinkles to concentrate in the upper portion of the arm.

To correct: Cut the sleeve along its whole length and open to the desired amount. The underarm will need to be lowered by the same amount at both the front and back side seams.

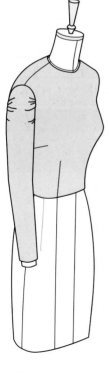

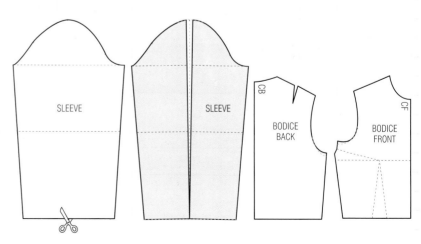

FITTING THE BUST

The following adaptations will help to correct fitting problems in the bust area.

HIGH BUST

The bust dart is positioned lower than the fullest part of the breast.
To correct: Realign the bust dart in line with the fullest part of the body.
Raise the tip of the waist dart the same amount as the bust dart has been raised.

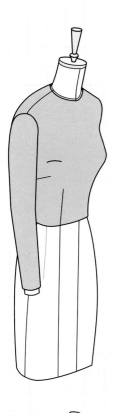

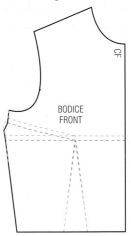

BODICE
FRONT

CF

LOW BUST

The bust dart is positioned higher than the fullest part of the breast.
To correct: Realign the bust dart in line with the fullest part of the body.
Lower the tip of the waist dart by the same amount as the bust dart has been lowered.

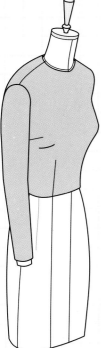

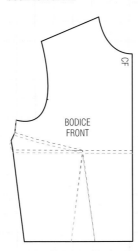

BODICE
FRONT

CF

DRAFTING TECHNIQUES

Fitting principles and pattern adjustments

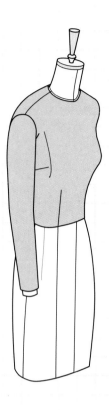

SMALL BUST

A small bust will cause the fitting muslin to collapse and crease over the bustline.
To correct: Cut your pattern piece into quarters through the center of the waist dart and bustline. Overlap the pieces to the required amount and straighten the shoulder seam.

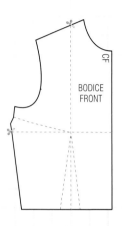 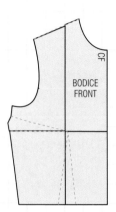

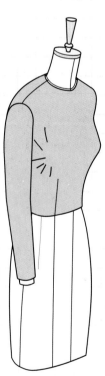

LARGE BUST

A large bust will cause the fitting muslin to strain across the bustline.
To correct: Cut your pattern piece into quarters through the center of the waist dart and bustline. Spread the pieces to the required amount and redraw the waist and bust darts, noting their new increased width at the base of the dart legs.

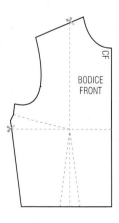 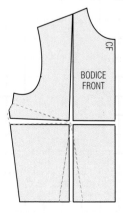

FITTING THE BACK

The following adaptations can resolve fitting problems across the back.

VERY ERECT BACK

This causes the garment to crumple and collapse across the shoulder blades.
To correct: Assess the depth of excess fabric through the upper back and lower the center back neckline and shoulder neck point by this amount. The shoulder point should now be raised by the same measurement.

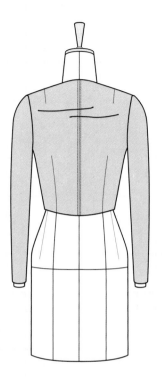

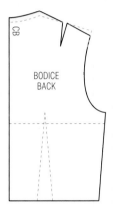

HIGH ROUNDED BACK

This will cause the garment to pull through the shoulders and arm holes.
To correct: Slash the pattern piece from the tip of the shoulder to the center back. Raise the released section to create more length through the entire back. Cut the panel through the neckline, pivoting the shoulder until the tips of the shoulder meet. This creates a dart at the neckline. The width of this dart in relation to fabric choice dictates whether this excess can be eased or darted.

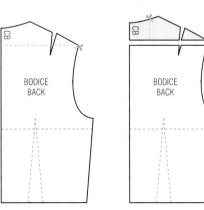

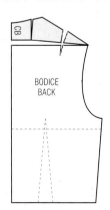

DRAFTING TECHNIQUES

Fitting principles and pattern adjustments

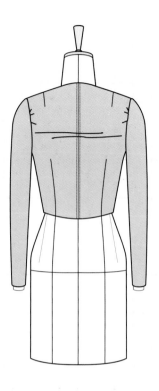

WIDE BACK

A fitting muslin without enough ease for a large back will exhibit wrinkles over the shoulders. The garment will also pull at the arm holes and, unless corrected, can cause a limited range of movement for the arms.
To correct: Cut the pattern piece as directed in the diagram, moving the released section to create more breadth across the upper back. Redraw the side seam and shoulder dart, noting the wider shoulder dart position.

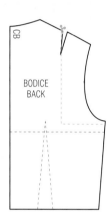 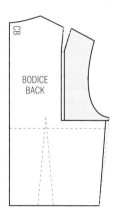

NARROW BACK

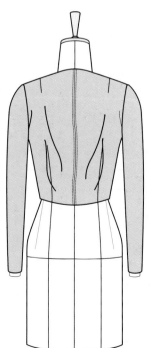

This will cause your fitting muslin to collapse over the shoulder blades.
To correct: Draw two lines, connecting each side of the shoulder dart to the base of the waist dart. Slash your pattern through one of these lines and overlap, pivoting slightly and obscuring both darts. This pattern piece does not now need a waist or shoulder dart, as all extra fullness has been removed.

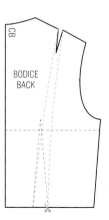 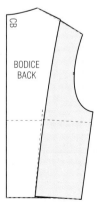

FITTING THE HIPS

The following adaptations can greatly improve the fit at the hips and buttocks for the individual figure.

LARGE BUTTOCKS

This will cause the skirt to ride up at both the hem and waist, distorting the side seams as the muslin creeps up over the buttocks.

To correct: Release the darts, allowing the center back waist to drop to a natural position. Re-pin the darts to fit the body profile. Transfer the changes to your paper pattern, raising the waistline and adding width at the side seam to fit.

SKIRT
BACK

FITTING A LARGE ABDOMEN

A large abdomen will cause the skirt to ride up at both the hem and waist. Side seams will begin to skew forward as the skirt pulls up across the hips to accommodate the abdomen.

To correct: Unpick the darts to release the center front waist. Pin the darts to fit the shape of the waist and transfer the alterations to your paper pattern, adding to the side seams if necessary.

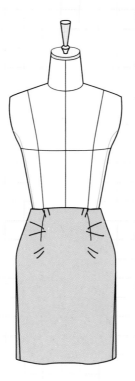

SKIRT
FRONT

DRAFTING TECHNIQUES
Fitting principles and pattern adjustments

CHAPTER 6:
RUB-OFF PATTERN DRAFTING

Although it is not widely publicized, rub-off pattern drafting, in which a pattern is traced or "lifted" from an existing item of clothing, is not uncommon within the fashion industry. This can be fueled by a desire to recreate a vintage find— the like of which is a staple of many design ranges.

There are two main methods of taking a pattern from an existing garment: the flat method, for predominantly flat garments, and the drape method, for more three-dimensional garments. For both methods, when all sections are traced, double-check seam lengths with the measurements of the original garment. A vintage piece is likely to have distorted with wear, so patterns should be trued up and then tested by producing a muslin.

THE FLAT METHOD

For mainly flat garments, such as a skirt, the simplest approach is to trace through the item directly onto pattern paper using a spiked tracing wheel. There are likely to be areas of suppression (darts, gathering, ease) within the garment that are slightly harder to transfer as they do not lay completely flat when pinned to paper. These may need to be estimated. If the piece can be unpicked to its component parts, the process becomes much simpler. For symmetrical garments, it is wise to trace just one half of the front and back; the piece can then be mirrored when cut. For demonstration purposes, the illustrations in this chapter show the pieces being traced on both sides.

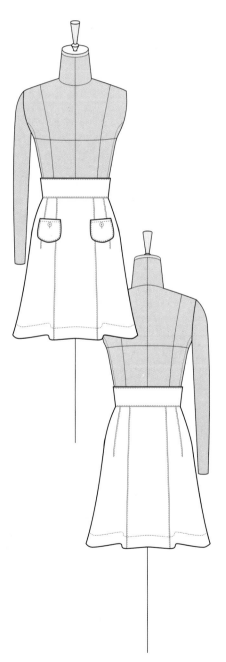

FLAT METHOD: RUB-OFF SKIRT

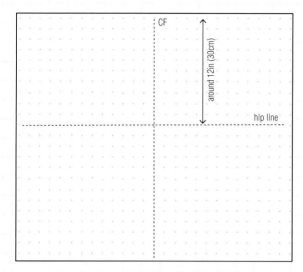

Cut a piece of pattern paper the length of the skirt plus an amount extra. In the center, mark a line straight down (CF); at about 12in (30cm) from the top, square across the hip line.

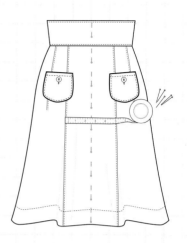

Find the CF of the skirt by measuring across and halving the amount, marking it with pins. Do this at spaced intervals down the top. If the skirt is symmetrical, you can measure from the seams rather than the edge.

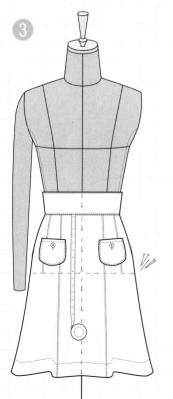

To find the hip line, put the skirt on the stand (or yourself) and pin a horizontal line at the widest part of the hip. This measurement should be around 8¼in (21cm) down from the waist.

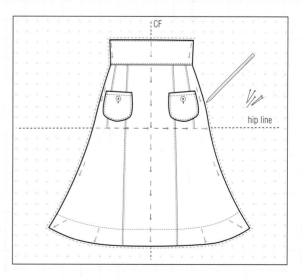

Place skirt on paper, matching CF and hip lines. Pin as flat as possible; areas that do not lie flat will have some form of shaping suppression. Trace around edge (side seams, hem, and waistline) with a pencil.

DRAFTING TECHNIQUES
Rub-off pattern drafting

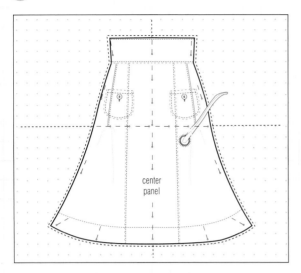

With a tracing wheel, trace through the seam at the waistline and central panel. Feel through to find seams of areas that may be covered by pockets, then trace through the pockets.

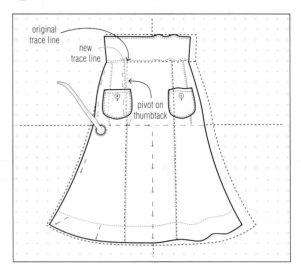

To find the shaping in the seam, on one side only, place a thumbtack or pin where the seam meets the hip line. Release the other side by taking out pins, then remove the pins above the hip line on both sides. Pivot so that the second panel lays flat. Pin this layer down and trace the new line.

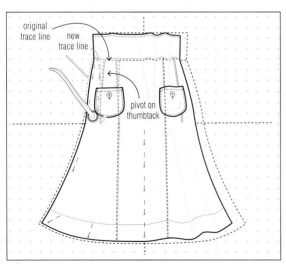

To find the dart shaping, move the thumbtack to where the dart hits the hip line and pivot so that the other top half of the second panel lays flat. Pin this layer down and trace a new line. Draw in a new side seam from waist to hip.

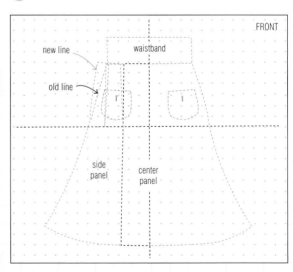

Unpin the skirt from the paper to reveal your trace markings. At this stage it is important that all lines are trued up and that right angles are correct. Curves should look good and flow without bumps. Trace the lines to the other side.

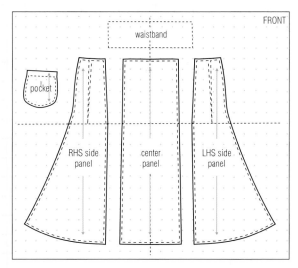

FRONT

waistband

pocket

RHS side panel | center panel | LHS side panel

Trace all sections. Apart from the waistband, add seam allowances, notches, and hem returns (if applicable) to all skirt panels. Include grainlines and pattern annotation on each piece.

 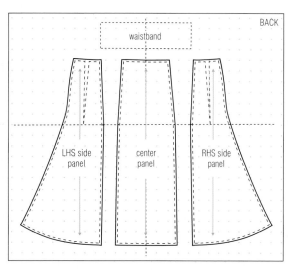

BACK

waistband

LHS side panel | center panel | RHS side panel

Repeat steps 1–9 for the back of the skirt. Make sure that connecting seams, such as the side seams, measure the same, allowing for ease and fullness that may be present. If not, true them up, referring back to the garment if needed.

 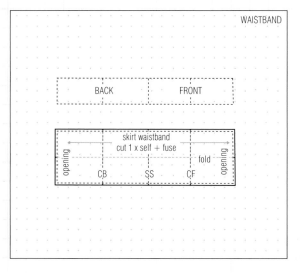

WAISTBAND

BACK | FRONT

skirt waistband
cut 1 x self + fuse

opening | CB SS CF | fold | opening

Create the waistband by attaching together the front and back sections, so that the opening is on the LHS. Mirror the section on the top edge, to create a folded waistband (this is only possible for straight waistbands; for curved waistbands, cut a pair). Add seam allowances.

 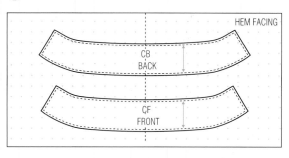

HEM FACING

CB BACK

CF FRONT

Create front and back hem facings using the traced panels, measuring the facing depth on the skirt. Add seam allowance.

DRAFTING TECHNIQUES
Rub-off pattern drafting

THE DRAPE METHOD

This technique is good for more complicated three-dimensional structures such as tailored jackets. Here, with the garment on a dress form, fabric is used to accurately copy the pattern sections. Being fabric, it is easier to mold it to the garment shape, and areas with precise shaping can be repeated. This is particularly helpful for areas with considerable ease, such as sleeveheads. The end result of this method is a muslin shell over the existing article. Once taken apart, the final pattern can be traced onto paper.

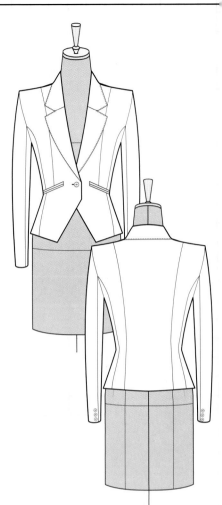

DRAPE METHOD: RUB-OFF JACKET

1

2

CF

around 12in (30cm)

waist to bust

around 8in (20cm)

bustline

waistline

grain

around 30in (75cm)

Put the jacket on the tailor's dummy or stand. Fasten the jacket, and flip the collar and rever up. With pins, around the garment mark the bustline (at the fullest point of the bust), the waistline, the CF, and CB.

Cut a piece of fabric the length of the jacket and around 30in (76cm) wide, or big enough to create the front panel, plus an amount extra. At around 8in (20cm) in from the LHS, draw a vertical line parallel to the grain; this is the CF. At a point 12in (30cm) down from the top of this line, square across the bustline. Measure the distance between the bustline and waistline on the jacket and mark a horizontal line at this point.

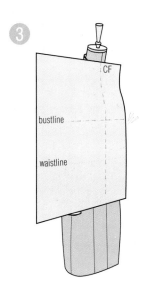

③ Place the cloth on the jacket, matching at the CF and bustline. Pin in place up CF and across bustline from the edge of the rever to the first seam/panel line.

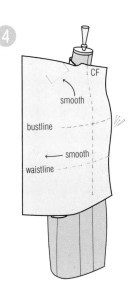

④ Pin waistline to first seam/panel line, smoothing out excess fabric. Smooth the cloth from bust to shoulder and pin the shoulder line at both neck and arm points. Draw in the shoulder seam.

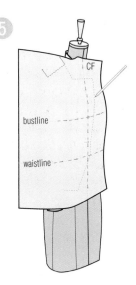

⑤ Feeling through the muslin to the jacket underneath, trace the front edge and rever with a chalk/clothmarking pencil, from where the first panel starts to the shoulder point on the neckline. Mark in button and buttonhole positions.

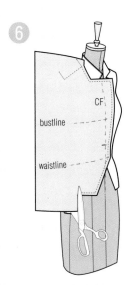

⑥ Cut off excess fabric at the front, leaving around ½in (1.5cm), removing unnecessary pins.

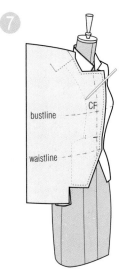

⑦ Mark the seam line of the first panel, including the pocket. Trim away excess as before, pinning at shoulder, bust, and waist (as shown) to hold panel in position.

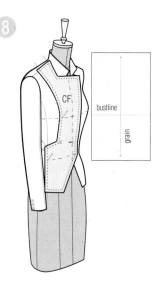

⑧ Cut a new piece of muslin, big enough to make the second panel, with extra. Mark the horizontal bustline around halfway down.

DRAFTING TECHNIQUES
Rub-off pattern drafting

9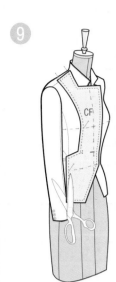

On the first cloth, clip into allowances at corners and along curves (as shown).

10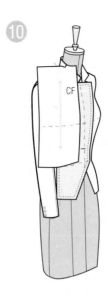

Place fabric onto jacket, matching bustline and ensuring that the grain remains at right angles. Pin in place.

11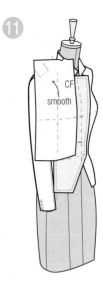

Smooth fabric from bust to shoulder, pin up grainline. Pin and mark shoulder line.

12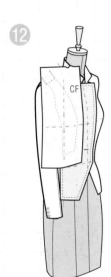

Feeling through the cloth to the jacket underneath, mark off the seams.

13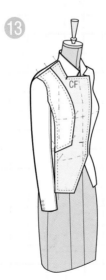

Trim away excess back to ½in (1.5cm), and clip.

14

Cut a new rectangle of muslin, big enough for the side panel. Mark on bustline and waistline (distance as set in step 1).

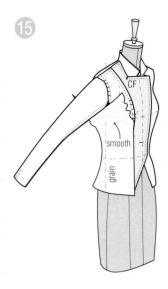

⑮ Place fabric onto jacket, matching waistline, while ensuring that the grainline is at right angles. Smooth any excess fabric from waist toward underarm. Once flat, pin at underarm point.

⑯ Mark seams onto muslin as before. To help trace the underarm, trim away and clip into excess fabric, making it lay flatter. Trim back excess, leaving ½in (1.5cm).

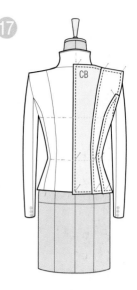

⑰ Repeat for back panels, as front.

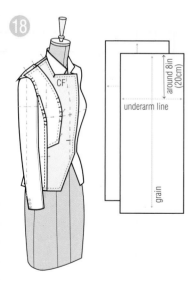

⑱ Prepare two pieces of muslin for the sleeve, approximately 30in (76cm) long by 15in (38cm). Mark a line down the center of each panel, squaring another line across 8in (20cm) from the top. On the jacket, pin a line straight down from the shoulder seam. Pin a line level to the underarm point around the sleeve.

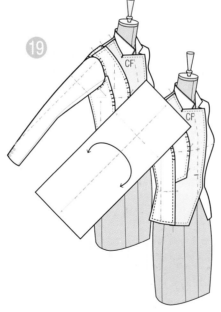

⑲ Place fabric on sleeve, matching central lines and underarm (bicep) line; pin down these lines. Wrap the fabric around the sleeve and pin at seams. Mark off seams and cuff.

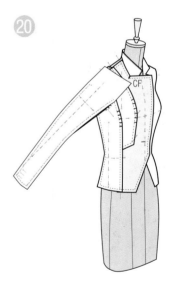

⑳ Trace off cuff and seams up to arm hole, marking notches at these points.

DRAFTING TECHNIQUES
Rub-off pattern drafting

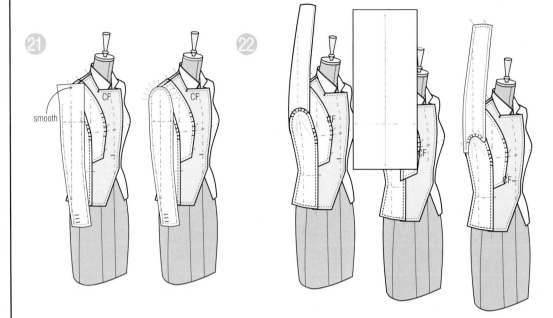

21 Smooth fabric up to sleevehead, pin at shoulder line (marking a notch there); then ease in excess evenly around the sleevehead (this is the ease the sleeve needs for a comfortable fit on the shoulder). Trim back to ½in (1.5cm) to remove unnecessary fabric; clip into allowances to help the sleevehead lay flat. Trace off sleevehead seam onto fabric.

22 Pin a line straight down from the underarm point on the sleeve; this will set the grain for the undersleeve. Take your second rectangle of muslin and pin in place to undersleeve, matching underarm line and grain. Trace off seams and cuff, trimming away excess to ½in (1.5cm).

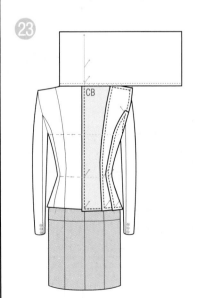

23 Cut a new piece of muslin for the collar, approximately 20in (50cm) wide and 8½in (21.5cm) deep. Draw a line ½in (1.5cm) up horizontally from the bottom edge; this amount is the allowance. Mark another line 4in (10cm) in from the left-hand edge; this is the CB and the grain of the collar section. Pin onto collar, matching CB and horizontal line with collar seam. Clip into allowance at ⅜–½in (1–1.5cm) intervals, so that the fabric can follow the form of the collar.

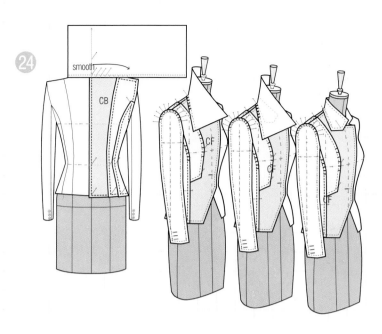

24

smooth

CB

CF

CF

CF

Curve and pin fabric around neckline to front of collar. The horizontal collar line will not follow the seam from the shoulder line on the front. Pin where it lays flat. Trace off seam line and collar edge onto fabric. Trim off excess back to ½in (1.5cm) and clip into it again to help it lay flat. Unpin all sections and trace off onto pattern paper, pinning and/or weighting the pieces in place. Make sure that all lines are trued up and that right angles are correct. To aid this, mark a grainline on the pattern paper first, then mark any important lines (such as the waist or bust) that square across, and match draped garment sections to this. Curves should look good and flow without bumps. Make sure that connecting seams, such as the side seams, measure the same (this does not apply to seams that contain ease or fullness). If not, true them up, referring back to the garment if needed.

1

1. Belted shirt dress.

(Photo credit: Simply Be)

DRAFTING TECHNIQUES

Rub-off pattern drafting

3

PATTERN DEVELOPMENT

CHAPTER 7: VOLUME AND SUPPRESSION

VOLUME

Even a basic close-fitting shape includes an amount of volume or "ease," which, as the term suggests, allows ease and movement within the garment to give a comfortable fit. This is even more relevant for over-garments, under which other clothes are worn.

When adding volume to a pattern piece, care must be taken where this is placed; extra flare can be given to the side seams, but if too much is given the garment becomes flat and wing-like. Volume is generally best spread evenly throughout the pattern piece in order to give a balanced and three-dimensional effect. Flare, too, must be added equally to front and back sections of a piece to keep the balance at the side seam; otherwise, the garment will twist or swing.

Once you understand the basic rules of adding fullness, you can play with controlling where the volume falls within a pattern piece. Whether you are creating a draped cowl or adding gather, volume is formed precisely at the points and direction that you slash and spread. This is especially relevant when asymmetrical flare is required.

The back is created in a similar manner: The back shoulder dart is closed, the bodice is divided, and fullness added. Ensure the side seam on the back bodice falls at the same angle as the front, or your garment will be skewed: to check, lay the back pattern over the front with shoulder neck points (SNP) touching and compare.

1. Roksanda Ilincic Astrae dress with added fullness at the waist gathered into a column skirt.

(Photo credit: Debenhams)

ADDING VOLUME TO BODICE WAIST

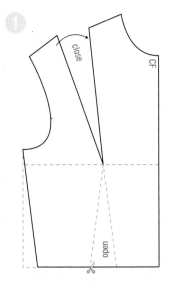

Remove and straighten the waist shaping on the side seams.

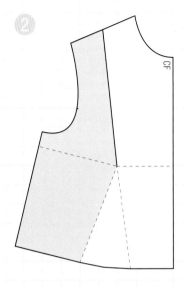

Pivot shoulder dart into waist dart.

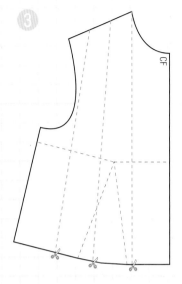

Divide shoulder line into three equal sections and waist into four; split pattern as shown in diagram.

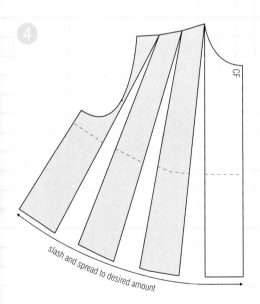

Spread sections as shown, opening equally to desired width.

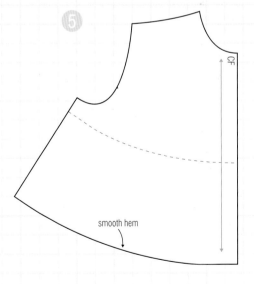

Curve off hem and shoulder; redraw bustline as a curve. Repeat for back as front.

PATTERN DEVELOPMENT

Volume and suppression

BISHOP SLEEVES

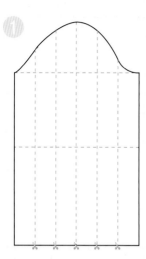

Divide elbow line by six and square off a line vertically, dividing sleeve into equal sections.

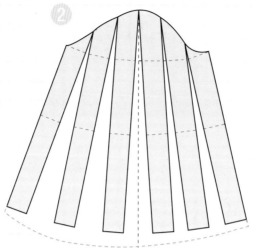

Slash and spread as shown, opening sections at wrist to the desired width.

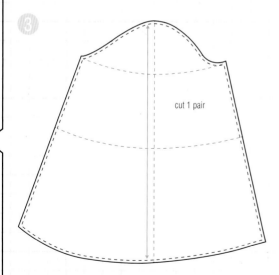

cut 1 pair

Add extra length as desired to sleeve at wrist (at least ¾in/2cm), to give a slight drop to sleeve. Curve off the sleevehead and redraw a new wrist line.

CLASSIC BISHOP SLEEVE

- To create a classic bishop sleeve (as shown in the diagram), add flare and length to the back half. This allows room for the elbow and creates a slight billow of volume at the back of the sleeve.

1. Star dress by Julien Macdonald with sheer bishop sleeve.

(Photo credit: Debenhams)

DECORATIVE EASE

- The excess fabric created at the crown can be further manipulated for decorative effect with the use of pleats, tucks, or gathers to suppress the fullness.

LEG-OF-MUTTON SLEEVE

A leg-of-mutton sleeve is characterized by a full upper sleeve that narrows over the forearm and wrist. Varying amounts of fullness in the upper part of the sleeve combined with the addition of height to the crown can be used to give a sleeve with a subtle gathered and puffed cap or something altogether more ostentatious.

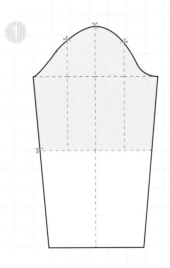

Take the basic sleeve block that has been slightly narrowed at the wrist line by 1¼–2in (3–5cm) (this manipulation can also be performed on the semi-fitted sleeve). Separate at the elbow and divide the upper portion of sleeve into four sections.

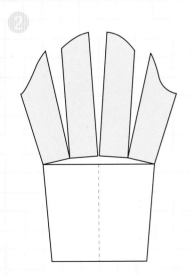

Slash and spread each upper section until the desired amount of fullness has been added.

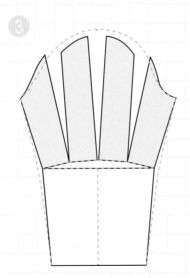

Raise the crown to the desired amount and redraw the front and back seams, creating a smooth curve from underarm to wrist.

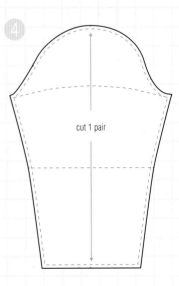

The finished pattern has seam allowance and annotation added.

cut 1 pair

PATTERN DEVELOPMENT
Volume and suppression

DRAPE AND COWL

Although unconstrained volume can be created by draping on the stand, the following examples show successful methods of creating flat pattern drape. In the diagrams on these pages, a cowl front is created in consecutive stages with progressively more volume added. In the Cowel Bodice diagrams, the bust dart is moved to the center front; this adaptation is used to create a garment with a minimal amount of added volume in which the waist dart is retained (1 and 2). The waist dart can be used to create increasingly more volume (3 and 4). In these, the drape begins to fall from the SNP (shoulder neck point), while in the Drape From Mid-Shoulder diagrams, the CF is lowered and the shoulder shortened to create a drape that falls from mid-shoulder. In this example, the neckline has been straightened, which enables this style to be finished with an all-in-one facing (3). This method can also be used in combination with the back sloper to create a garment with a draped back.

CUTTING BIAS SHAPES

Cutting bias shapes on a fold is not recommended; the pattern piece should be mirrored for the most successful cut.

1. Tunic with deep cowl falling from shoulder neck point.

(Photo credit: La Redoute)

2. Deep-cowl cardigan.

(Photo credit: Mint Velvet)

COWEL BODICE

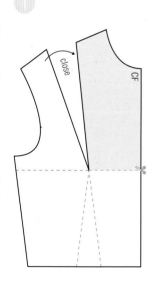

Cut along chest line and close bust dart to transfer dart excess to CF.

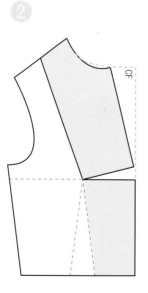

Extend the center front and connect to neckline.

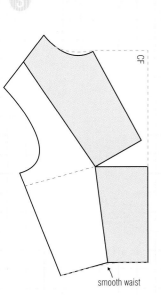

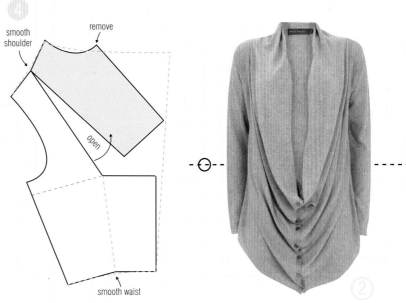

Closing the waist dart adds further depth to the cowl; again extend the CF line and connect to neckline.

Pivoting the upper section adds an increased amount of fullness into the cowl—note how the new CF line is now angled.

DRAPE FROM MID-SHOULDER

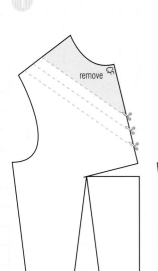

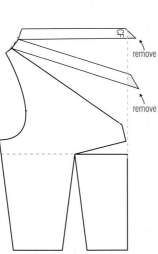

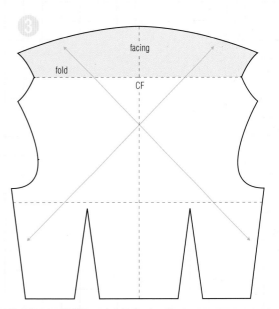

Mark and slash red lines as shown.

Extend CF line and pivot released sections until uppermost segment runs at a 90-degree angle to CF.

The finished pattern piece with an all-in-one facing.

PATTERN DEVELOPMENT

Volume and suppression

GATHERING

Gathers are a form of constrained fullness or suppression. They are produced by drawing up a set measurement of fabric to fit a smaller area. Gathers can be ordered and spread evenly, or bunched and irregular. The type of fabric used will vary the effect: soft materials will drape; crisp fabrics will hold form and billow.

When creating gathered patterns, a ratio needs to be specified (for example, 2:1) for the amount that the gathered section needs to be drawn up to fit the smaller section. This simplifies the pattern for the machinist.

Gathers can utilize the dart shaping already present in a basic block, or extra fullness can be added by slashing and spreading the pattern in the direction of the required volume.

1. Lace skater dress
with Peter Pan collar.

(Photo credit: Missguided.co.uk)

2. Luxury ruche dress with
asymmetrical gathered panels.

(Photo credit: Freemans)

SEWING GATHERS

With a large stitch length, sew two lines, one just in from the stitch line on the seam allowance, and a second ¼in (6mm) in. Do not back-tack, and leave thread ends long. By pulling the thread ends of the bobbin thread, gather the seam allowance to the ratio set on the pattern, making sure that gathers are spread evenly—using two stitch lines helps with this. Pin the gathered piece onto the smaller piece and, with a normal stitch length, sew the seam. Overlock the raw edges, and press the seam allowances in the direction away from the gathers. Gathered areas can be pressed by opening up the area flat and pressing as far into the gather as possible. Do not press over the gathers, as they will flatten, spoiling the effect.

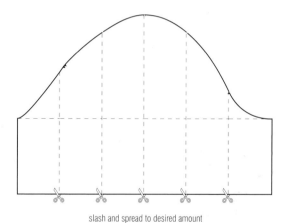

slash and spread to desired amount

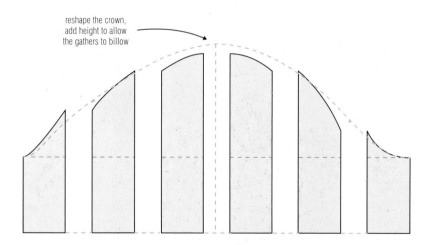

reshape the crown, add height to allow the gathers to billow

PATTERN DEVELOPMENT
Volume and suppression

PLEATS

Pleats are pressed folds that suppress volume through part or all of a garment section. They can be used singularly or repeated; allowed to open and fall freely, or stitched down and released at a specific point. Such a pleat is used at the back of a jacket lining to give an extra amount of volume across the shoulders for a comfortable fit.

Pleats can give flare and "swing" to a garment, and enable a large amount of volume to be present while still having a fitted silhouette. Pleating can utilize a lot of fabric: a typical pleat ratio is 3:1. Fold lines must be marked accurately, and match points notched.

Certain fabrics pleat more easily than others; materials with a polyester content can be permanently heat-set, whereas other synthetics such as acrylic do not have good pleat retention.

It is advisable to hem any areas before pleating, as hemming afterward will spoil the pleating. Companies specializing in pleating are able to produce an amazing variety of intricate pleat designs, which appear more like paper origami than fabric.

TYPES OF PLEATS

Knife pleats: these lay in one direction only.

fold | placement line | fold | placement line | fold | placement line | fold | placement line | fold | placement line

1. Tailored linen dress with scalloped neckline and inverted-box-pleat skirt.

(Photo credit: ASOS)

Box pleats/inverted box pleats: These lay in two opposite directions. Box pleats have pleats that turn away from one another, while inverted box pleats face one another.

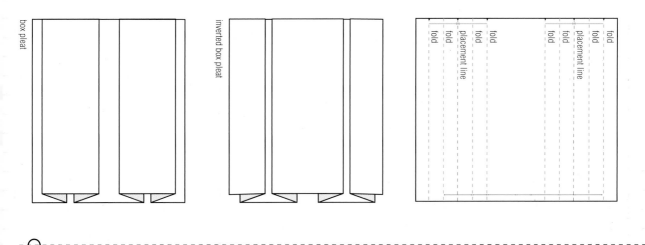

MIRRORING A PLEAT

This ensures that the pleat excess maintains the same profile as the seam allowance after construction. Add pleat width to pattern, then fold paper, placing pleat excess in desired direction. Trace the yoke profile to the folded pleat. Open out the pattern piece, noting the extended profile of the pleat.

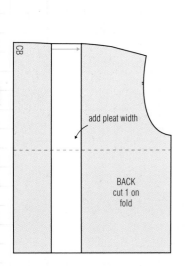

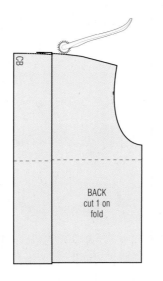

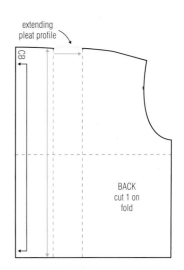

CHAPTER 8: SLEEVES

In this chapter, a range of sleeve techniques is provided to add variety to your designs. A well-set-in sleeve will frame a garment, and care and attention should be shown at the construction phase to ensure consistency. Refer to the diagram on p. 44 for a reminder as to the correct method of construction.

After pattern manipulation is complete, measure the front and back arm hole and crown, making a note of these figures on your patterns. You will note that the crown measurement is greater than that of the combined arm hole; this is to be expected, as this ease is an allowance for the fullness of the upper arm and shoulder. Depending on fabric choice, it may be necessary to reduce this ease—refer to the fitting and alteration technique on p. 87 to complete this.

1. Chiffon blouse with oversized kimono-style inset sleeves.
(Photo credit: ASOS)

2. Button-front shirt with bishop-style sleeve gathered at the wrist.
(Photo credit: Lipsy)

116–117

DECORATIVE ELBOW DART

The elbow dart can be further manipulated for decorative effect. Consider tucks, pleats, or a series of pin tucks to suppress this fullness.

SEMI-FITTED SLEEVE

This sleeve could be considered a block in its own right; it may be worth copying onto card to save time manipulating the basic sleeve block if used frequently. As its name suggests, the semi-fitted sleeve gives a closer fit at the wrist, as well as creating a dart at the elbow.

1¼in (3cm)   1¼in (3cm)

BASIC SLEEVE

Measure in from the wristline 1¼in (3cm) and connect this point to the underarm point.

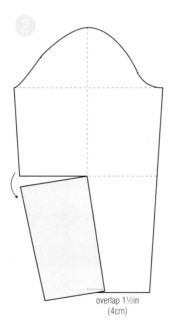

overlap 1½in (4cm)

Cut along the center line of the sleeve up to the elbow line and again from the elbow line to the center to release the back section of the sleeve below the elbow. Pivot this section to create an overlap of approximately 1½in (4cm) at the wristline, thus creating a new dart at the elbow.

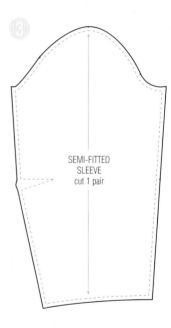

SEMI-FITTED SLEEVE cut 1 pair

Make a new copy of your sleeve, reducing the elbow dart by half its length. Add seam allowances and pattern annotation.

PATTERN DEVELOPMENT
Sleeves

RAGLAN SLEEVES

Often associated with sportswear, providing a comfortable fit and offering a free range of movement, this adaptation is particularly suitable for activewear garments and knitwear patterning. This style combines the shoulder section of the front and back bodice patterns with the sleeve. In its simplest form, a diagonal seam runs from the neckline to the underarm: a baseball shirt is a good example of this.

A raglan sleeve can be drafted in one piece, with a dart at the sleevehead to provide suppression at the shoulder, or it can be converted into a two-piece sleeve by separating the sleeve on the center line and adding seam allowances. While the drafting procedure may seem a little tricky to the beginner, it is easier to construct than a set-in sleeve.

The first stage is to temporarily move the back shoulder dart; the front bust dart will also need to be moved for the duration of this drafting process. Next, trace around the basic sleeve sloper and lower the crown to remove excess ease from the sleevehead (see p. 87).

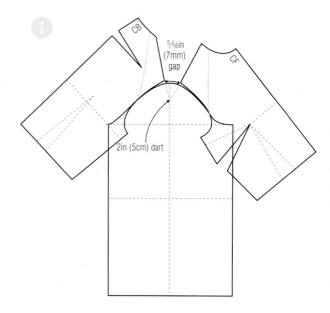

Lay the front and back bodice slopers onto the traced sleeve, matching balance points but leaving a ⁵⁄₁₆in (7mm) gap between the SNP and center of the sleeve. Create a dart at the sleevehead of approximately 2in (5cm) to give a smooth run at the shoulder. Draw in your required seam lines, ensuring they blend into the bodice and sleeve at the balance points.

Trace off new pieces, closing the temporary back shoulder dart and bust dart if necessary, and add seam allowances and pattern annotation.

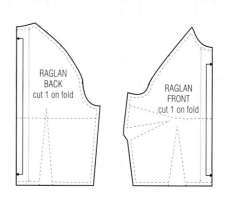

Repeat step 2 for the raglan back and front, tracing off new pieces, closing the temporary back shoulder dart and bust dart if necessary, and add seam allowances and pattern annotation.

CAPES

Cape patterns can be generated from your basic blocks in much the same way as the flat collars described on p. 125. Before completing the cape exercises, the bodice and sleeve blocks can be adapted to centralize the shoulder line.

GENERATING A CAPE BLOCK

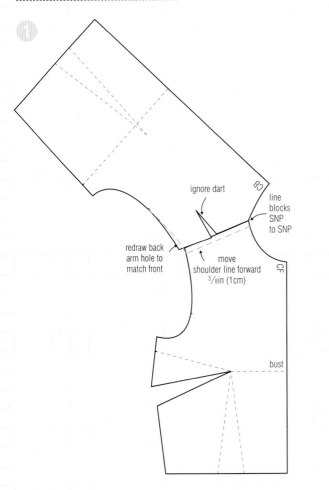

ignore dart

CB

line
blocks
SNP
to SNP

redraw back
arm hole to
match front

move
shoulder line forward
³⁄₈in (1cm)

CF

bust

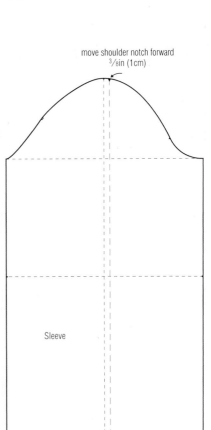

move shoulder notch forward
³⁄₈in (1cm)

Sleeve

Lay front and back blocks together with SNP touching, and redraw the back shoulder line ³⁄₈in (1cm) forward. Redraw the back arm hole to create a smooth run with front arm hole and ignore the back shoulder dart.

Although the sleeve block is not necessary for the cape drafting procedures, this adaptation can also be used in conjunction with the raglan drafting method described above; to this end, the shoulder notch is moved forward ³⁄₈in (1cm) to match the newly situated shoulder line.

PATTERN DEVELOPMENT

Sleeves

CAPE WITH FULL FLUTED HEM

To create a cape of any length with a full fluted hem:

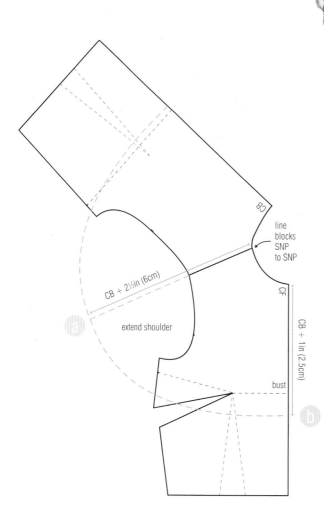

Lay patterns together with front and back SNP touching and mark the desired length at CB. Extend shoulder line measurement using CB measurement plus 2½in (6cm) (a) and mark CF at CB measurement plus 1in (2.5cm) (b). Connect these points to create the outer (hem) edge of your cape, as shown in diagram. The cape can be cut in one or a seam can be created at the shoulder line, aligning grain to CB and CF.

1. Sequin cape with full-flared hem.

(Photo credit: Internacionale)

2. Canvas and merino cape with reduced hem.

(Photo credit: Land's End)

CAPE WITH LESS FLARE IN HEM

To create a cape of any length with less flare in the hem:

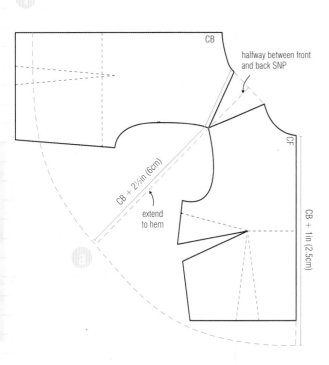

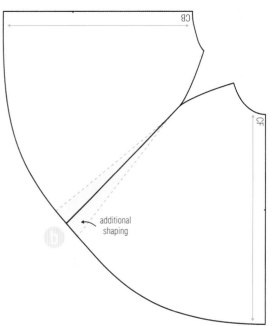

Align blocks with shoulder points touching and pivot SNP until blocks are positioned at a 90-degree angle to each other. Again, mark CB length and determine shoulder seam and CF length using the measurements described above. Trace the front and back draft, ensuring that side seam measurements match (a).

Fullness can be further constrained at the side seam (this additional shaping is shown in gray on the diagram) (b).

ALL-IN-ONE CAP SLEEVE

To create a short sleeve cut in one with the main body of the garment:

Raise the shoulder line by ⅜in (1cm) (a). Extend the shoulder line and connect to the bodice side seams, marking the end of the sleeve opening with a notch (b).

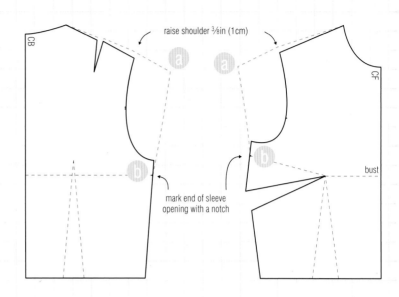

raise shoulder ⅜in (1cm)

CB

CF

bust

mark end of sleeve opening with a notch

TWO-PIECE SLEEVE

A two-piece sleeve follows the natural curve of the arm and can be used to great effect on fitted or tailored garments. This sleeve can be cut using the basic sleeve sloper or the semi-fitted sleeve.

Omit stage 1 if your starting point is the basic sleeve sloper.

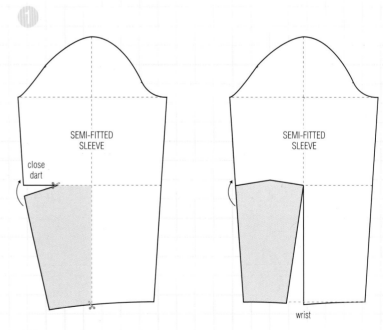

SEMI-FITTED SLEEVE

SEMI-FITTED SLEEVE

close dart

wrist

Fold out the elbow dart and straighten the wrist.

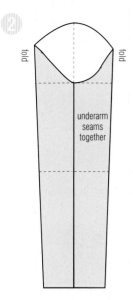

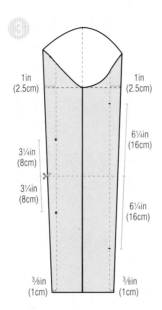

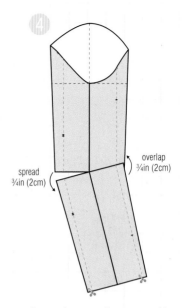

Fold sleeve so that the underarm seams touch the center line, and pin or tape into position. Measure 1in (2.5cm) in from fold at the bicep level and ³⁄₈in (1cm) at wrist. Connect these two points with a straight line to create the new seams for your two-piece sleeve. Now mark notches either side of the elbow, approximately 3¼in (8cm) on the back sleeve and 6¼in (16cm) on the front.

Cut through the elbow line, pivoting the released section downward by ¾in (2cm); tape or pin into place. Notice how the back seam is now longer and the front seam is shorter: this discrepancy will be eased and stretched during construction.

Cut up the seam lines created in step 3 to separate your sleeve into two pieces, opening out the fold created in step 2, to create a top sleeve and the undersleeve.

Add pattern annotation and seam allowances and mark the areas to be stretched or eased.

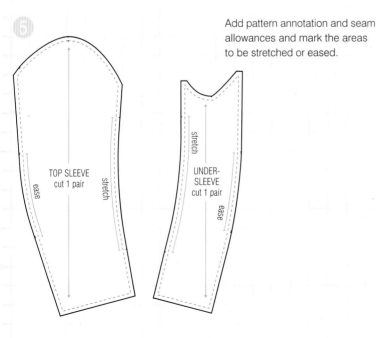

CHAPTER 9: COLLARS

Before drafting any of the following collars, lower or adjust the neckline as the individual design dictates. Using the tape measure on its side, measure the neckline, making a note of the complete and individual front and back neckline measurements.

It should be noted, as a general principle, that the length of the outer edge of a collar dictates its resting position in a finished garment. A reduction in length encourages the collar to sit higher on the shoulder line, creating a roll at the neckline. To see this principle in action, pin small darts or make slashes regularly around the leaf edge of a sample collar to observe the effects. You will notice that as the roll of a collar increases, the width of the collar may also need to be extended to accommodate this.

There are three basic types of collars: stand-up, shirt, and flat.

If a top collar and undercollar are required, add 1–2in (2.5–5cm) to the neck and outer edge of the top collar. This addition will ensure the top collar rolls under out of sight, so the bagged-out edge does not show upon wear.

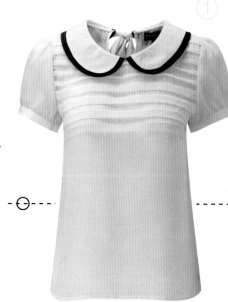

LOWERING NECKLINES

Lowering the neckline by approximately $^3/_8$in (1cm) at the center front to nothing at the shoulder neck point (SNP) can improve the fit of most types of collar and will also avoid the collar feeling restrictive upon wear.

CUTTING COLLARS

Collars can be cut on a fold, or the draft can be mirrored and cut on a single layer. Tracing and cutting your finished collar draft onto a folded piece of paper will speed up the mirroring process.

1. Top with Peter Pan collar.

(Photo credit: Fever)

FLAT COLLARS

An important point to remember when drafting flat collars is that the greater
the overlap at the shoulders, the more the leaf edge of a flat collar will be reduced.
When drafting a flat collar for a pattern of your own design that has a bust dart
situated at the shoulder or neckline, temporarily move or close this dart while
you draft the collar. (This principle does not apply to the back shoulder dart.)

PETER PAN COLLAR

A Peter Pan collar is a rounded, flat collar without a stand, although this
drafting method can be used to great effect with any shaped collar of your
choice. The example below will give a collar with very little roll at the neckline:
Increase the overlap at the shoulder to create a collar with more roll.

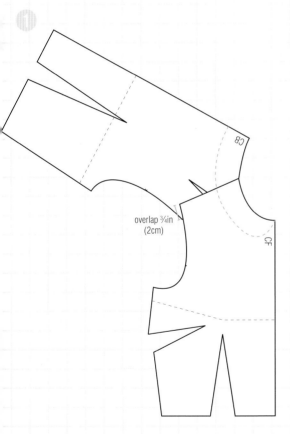

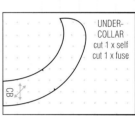

Trace a copy of your collar, adding
seam allowances and annotation
in the usual manner. Remember the
undercollar will also require interlining
or fusing, so ensure you add this
instruction to the pattern piece.

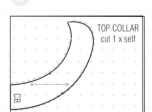

Lower the neckline first if necessary. Lay the front and back pattern pieces together
with the shoulder neck points touching and the shoulder points overlapping by
approximately ¾in (2cm). Draw the desired collar shape, ensuring you mark notches
at the shoulder seams.

Make another copy of your collar.
Before adding seam allowances, add
an extra ⅛in (3mm) to its leaf and neck
edges, as shown in the diagram, to
ensure that your top collar will roll
neatly and will not expose any of
the bagged-out seam.

PATTERN DEVELOPMENT
Collars

ETON COLLAR

An Eton collar is very similar to a Peter Pan collar; it is a flat collar with no
stand but has a flat leaf edge and sits a little higher and wider on the neckline.
The example below will give a collar with a partial roll at the neckline: increase
the overlap at the shoulder as your design dictates.

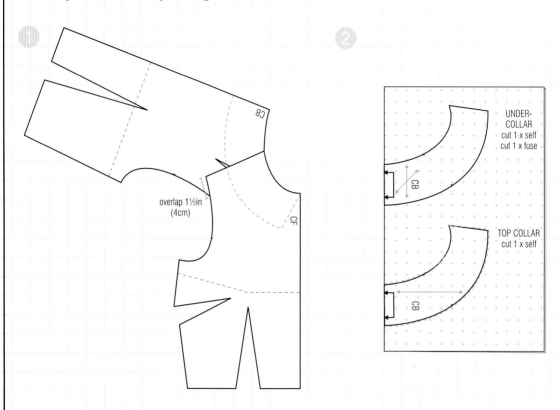

Lower the neckline first if necessary. Lay the front and back
pattern pieces together with the shoulder neck points touching
and the shoulder points overlapping by approximately 1½in
(4cm). Draw the desired collar shape, ensuring you mark
notches at the shoulder seams.

Follow Peter Pan instructions from step 2 (see p. 125).

MANDARIN COLLAR

A Mandarin collar is simple band collar that has been shaped at the neck edge to follow the profile of the neck. The following example exhibits the minimum of shaping; a deeper collar may require more. Adjust as your design dictates.

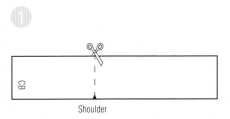

Draft a rectangle using the combined front and back measurements in length and approximately 1³⁄₈in (3.5cm) in height. Mark the shoulder notch position using half the back measurement as a guide. Mark a dashed line vertically through the collar at the shoulder notch.

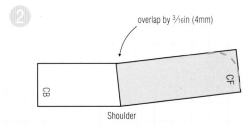

overlap by ³⁄₁₆in (4mm)

Slash the collar draft along the dashed line and pivot the upper edge, overlapping pieces by ³⁄₁₆in (4mm). Shape the center front of the collar if required.

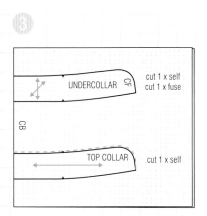

Trace two copies of your manipulated pattern, smoothing the overlapping lines to create smooth continuous curves. Add seam allowances and pattern annotation, remembering to add a turning allowance to the top collar.

1. Dress with Eton collar. (Photo credit: ASOS)

PATTERN DEVELOPMENT
Collars

SHIRT COLLARS

TWO-PIECE SHIRT COLLAR

This traditional two-piece collar is drafted with the Mandarin collar in the previous example as a basis. Lower the neckline ¼ in (6mm) at center front.

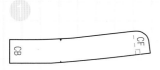

Follow stage 1 of Mandarin collar draft; this will become the stand for your two-piece collar. At a 90-degree angle from the CF add a button-stand extension if required.

Draft the collar fall, squaring from the CB and using the upper edge of the Mandarin collar as a guide.

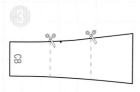

Divide the collar into thirds.

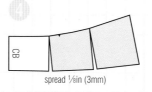

spread ⅛in (3mm)

Spread each collar section ⅛in (3mm).

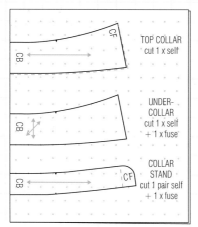

TOP COLLAR
cut 1 x self

UNDER-COLLAR
cut 1 x self
+ 1 x fuse

COLLAR STAND
cut 1 pair self
+ 1 x fuse

Trace two copies of your manipulated pattern. Add seam allowances and pattern annotation, remembering to add a bagging-out allowance to the top collar.

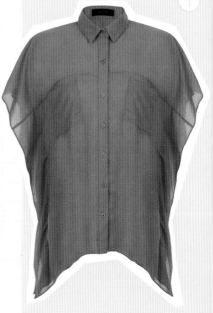

1. Oversize blouse with two-piece shirt collar.

(Photo credit: Fashion Union)

REVER COLLAR

Follow this drafting method for high rever styles that break above the bustline. For a rever on a low neckline, ensure that excess ease is removed from the neckline as shown on p. 59.

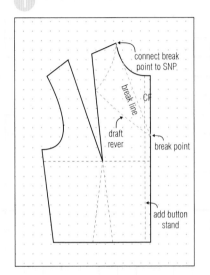

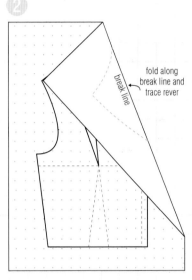

Add a button stand to the bodice draft and draft the rever shape. Connect base of rever to shoulder neck point with a straight dashed line and label the break point.

Fold paper along the break line and trace through the rever shape.

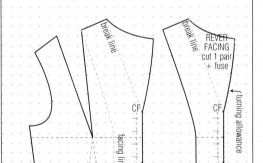

Mark the facing position and trace off a copy, adding a turning allowance to the lead edge of the facing.

2. Dress with contrast rever.

(Photo credit: Dunnes)

| PATTERN DEVELOPMENT |
| Collars |

CHAPTER 10: WAISTBANDS AND CUFFS

WAISTBANDS

Waistbands are used to finish and support the waist of a garment. Select from the following techniques, depending on the desired placement in relation to the waistline.

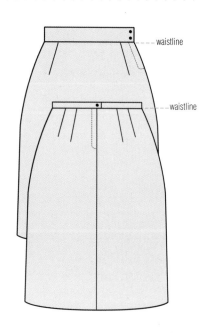

waistline

waistline

STRAIGHT WAISTBAND ON THE WAIST

A straight waistband is the simplest of waistbands; it can be used successfully if set on the waistline and drafted in widths between 1 and 3¼in (2.5–8cm). This drafting method is also suitable for use as a channel for an elastic or a ribbed waistband or a band cuff.

The instructions below apply to both a wide waistband (as shown in top diagram right and upper diagram below), or to a narrow waistband (as shown in bottom diagram right and lower diagram below). Measure the waistline of your pattern, remembering to subtract the total dart excess. Draft a rectangle to this measurement × double the width of the finished waistband. (If fabric economy is a consideration, draft pattern to single waistband width and cut 1 × lining, 1 × self.) Mark CB, CF, and side seam with notches. Mark the fold line with a dashed line. If required, add an under-wrap and mark button and buttonhole position. Add seam allowances and pattern annotation.

WIDE WAISTBAND WITH SIDE-SEAM OPENING

CB	fold	CF
cut 1 × self + fuse		

NARROW WAISTBAND WITH CENTER-BACK OPENING

CB	fold	CF	CB
cut 1 × self + fuse			

waistline

SHAPED WAISTBAND BELOW THE WAIST

Waistbands set below the waistline require shaping to fit the contours of the body and should be cut singly and fused.

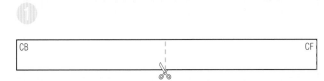

Trim required amount from waistline of skirt pattern and record this lowered waist measurement. Using the general (or personal) waist measurement, make a straight waistband as described opposite.

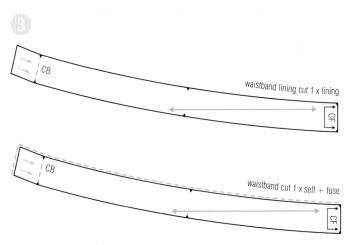

Slash at CB, CF, and side seam, spreading the lower edge until it is the same length as the newly created low waistline measurement recorded in stage 1.

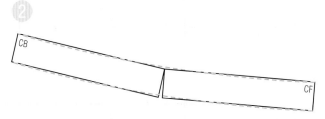

Smooth off shaped waistband and add button stand if required. Add seam allowances and pattern annotation.

SHAPED WAISTBAND ABOVE THE WAIST

Waistbands set above the waistline require shaping to fit the body.
Shaped waistbands need to be cut singly and fused.

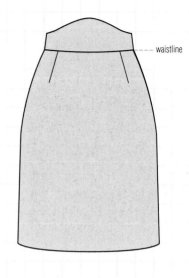

waistline

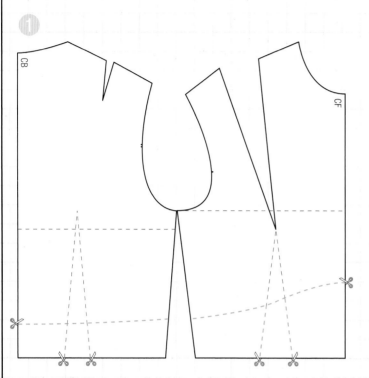

Trace shaped bodice block and draw in desired
waistband. Cut out waistband and close darts.

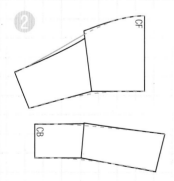

Trace around pattern and create a continuous line, smoothing
closed dart legs. Draft button-wrap if required, then add seam
allowance and pattern annotation.

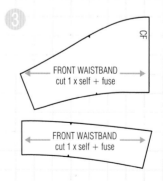

FRONT WAISTBAND
cut 1 x self + fuse

FRONT WAISTBAND
cut 1 x self + fuse

Trace another copy, adding ⅛in (3mm) for turning. Further
shaping may be required at side seams; ensure that you are
aware of the measurement of both skirt and sloper waistlines to
assess the required reduction. Side seams can be joined and
blended for a CB or CF opening.

waistline

LOW-RISE WAISTBAND

Only very narrow straight waistbands should be drafted using this method: maximum width 1in (2.5cm). For deeper waistbands, use the shaped waistband method described on p. 131. You may also want to consider removing ¼in (6mm) from the front and back waistline side seams, running smoothly to the hip for an improved fit. Mark lowered waistline on skirt pattern 2–2½in (5–6cm) below waistline and create a straight waistband to fit.

ALTERNATIVE WAIST FINISHES

Waistbands can also be finished with a waistband facing or bias binding.

1. Paper-bag waistline skirt with contrast waistband.
(Photo credit: Very)

2. Skirt with below-the-waist shaped waistband.
(Photo credit: Littlewoods)

CUFFS

Before cuffs are added, the sleeve guard or relevant opening must be completed. Cuffs can be attached before or after the sleeve is sewn into the arm hole, depending on the type of sleeve and the desired construction process. However, remember that most cuff types can only be attached after the underarm seam has been sewn.

SHIRT CUFF

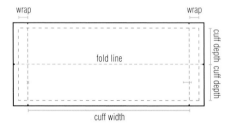

Plan cuff to desired measurements; if required, add an over- and/or underlap. Mark the extension with a notch if applicable.

1. Holly Willoughby large-collar blouse.
(Photo credit: Very)

SHAPED CUFF

Due to its curved profile, a shaped cuff cannot be cut on the fold. To this end, plan cuff to desired measurements, adding an over- or underlap if required. Trace another copy, add a turning allowance to the outer edges, and label it "top cuff."

Add interfacing to provide stability and sew the pieces together. Prepare the cuff for bagging out by snipping the curve, cutting out triangles of fabric to remove bulk, and grading the seam allowances to reduce excess.

ATTACHING A BAGGED-OUT SECTION

The following construction method describes the method of construction for a lapped cuff with an opening, but the technique is much the same to attach any bagged-out shape such as a collar or waistband.

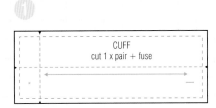

CUFF
cut 1 x pair + fuse

Plan cuff to desired measurements; if required, add an over- and/or underlap. Mark the extension with a notch if applicable.

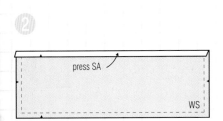

press SA

WS

Press SA on one long side of cuff piece to WS.

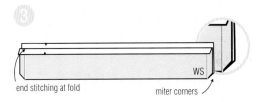

end stitching at fold

WS

miter corners

Fold the cuff in half, RS together, and sew both short sides. Stop stitching at SA fold. Miter corners to reduce bulk. Bag out cuff and press.

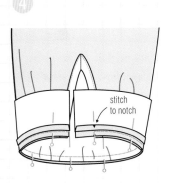

stitch to notch

Place the unpressed cuff edge to the inside of the sleeve hem, lining up the notch with the opening edge. RS of the cuff fabric should be facing the WS of the sleeve fabric. Sew cuff to sleeve, stopping stitching at extension notch and ensuring stitching does not catch the folded SA.

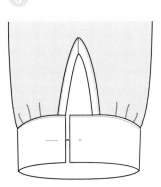

Turn cuff to the RS and press the seam down inside the cuff. Trim any areas of excess fabric that may cause unnecessary bulk. Close the cuff edge with an edgestitch through all layers. All raw seam edges will be enclosed in the cuff. Topstitch the cuff if desired.

PATTERN DEVELOPMENT
Waistbands and cuffs

CHAPTER 11:
OPENINGS AND FASTENINGS

OPENINGS

Areas of the garment such as the neckline or the cuff may require additional openings to allow for the head or hand to pass through. For dresses, skirts, and pants, this opening commonly goes to the hip line. If an opening in an existing seam is not possible or desired, an opening can be created with a placket. A placket is typically a doubled fabric section that supports button fastenings, and is usually found on the CF and cuff of a shirt. When considering openings, you must also decide the methods by which they, in turn, are closed. The variety of closures or fastenings is covered in the next section.

ALL-IN-ONE BUTTON STAND

An all-in-one button stand can be used on reversible fabrics. As you can see from the construction diagram, this button stand is created in one piece so the wrong side of the fabric is folded back, and on view (as part of the outer). The right-hand side (RHS) and left-hand side (LHS) of this opening are drafted in the same manner, but, as you will see from the diagram, they are not sewn in the same way.

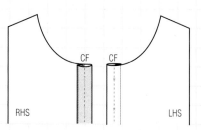

RHS   CF   CF   LHS

DRAFTING AN ALL-IN-ONE BUTTON STAND

① ② ③

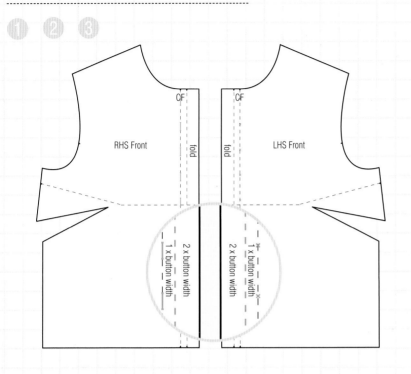

RHS: from the center front draw a dashed line 1 x the width of the button. Mark this line as "fold" (1).

RHS: from the fold line, draw another line at 2 x the width of the button (2).

LHS: repeat steps 1 and 2 as for RHS (3).

④ ⑤

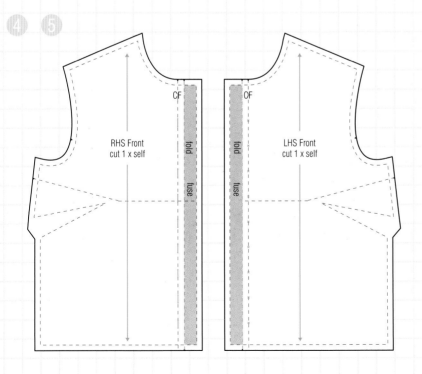

Mark button and buttonhole positions (4).

Add seam allowances and pattern annotation, noting areas to fuse (5).

PATTERN DEVELOPMENT
Openings and fastenings

SEPARATE BUTTON STAND

This type of button stand is suitable for fabrics that cannot be turned to show the wrong side of the fabric due to obvious differences between the different sides of the fabric. This type of button stand would also be used on a garment style with a yoke seam, which would otherwise bisect the button stand.

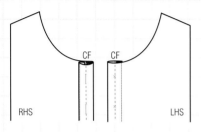

DRAFTING A SEPARATE BUTTON STAND

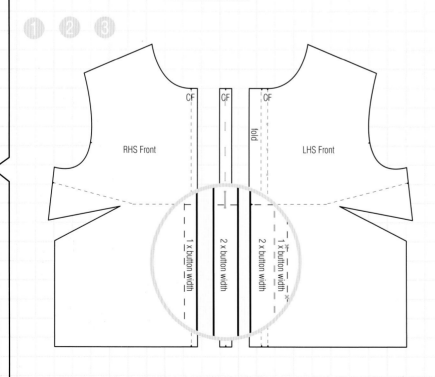

RHS: from the center front, draw a dashed line 1 x the width of the button and mark this line as "fold" (1).

LHS: from the center front, draw a dashed line 1 x the width of the button and mark this line as "fold" (2).

LHS: from the fold line, draw another at 2 x the width of the button (3).

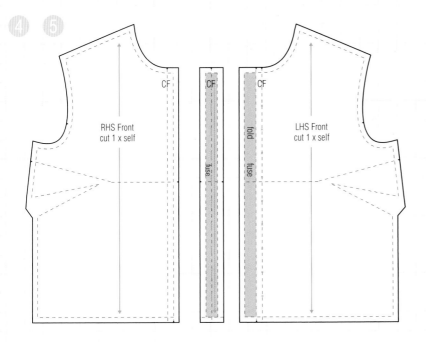

RHS Front
cut 1 x self

CF

CF

fuse

fold

fuse

CF

LHS Front
cut 1 x self

Mark button and buttonhole positions (4).

Add seam allowances and pattern annotation, noting areas to fuse (5).

MARKING BUTTONHOLES

Buttons should be selected appropriately for the situation, and of a suitable size for the location and thickness of fabric. Buttons can be either sew-through or with a shank; sew-through buttons tend to be better for thinner fabrics, whereas the shank allows for thicker materials.

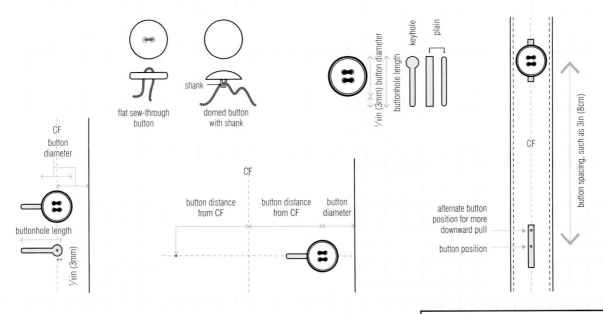

flat sew-through button

shank

domed button with shank

1/8in (3mm) button diameter

buttonhole length

keyhole

plain

CF
button diameter

buttonhole length

1/8in (3mm)

CF

button distance from CF

button distance from CF

button diameter

CF

alternate button position for more downward pull

button position

button spacing, such as 3in (8cm)

PATTERN DEVELOPMENT

Openings and fastenings

SHIRT SLEEVE PLACKET (SLEEVE GUARD)

A sleeve placket allows for an opening at the cuff of a shirt. There are many
variations of placket; common to all of them is the creation of an overlap
(the placket), which is the more visible part, and the underlap, which is hidden.

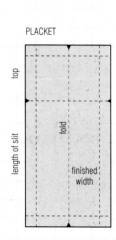

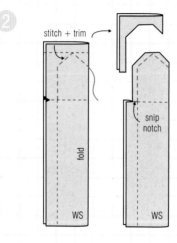

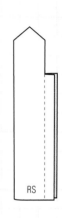

To draft the placket, decide the length
needed for the slit opening (around
4¼in/11cm). Draw a rectangle this
height plus around 1¼in (3cm) for the
top of the placket; the width should be
twice the desired finished width of the
placket (finished width say, ¾in/2cm).
Add ½in (1.2cm) seam allowances to
the bottom and top edges, and ¼in
(6mm) to each side.

Fold the placket in half, right sides
facing, and pin. Mark the desired shape
of the top of the placket (i.e. rounded,
pointed, squared) and stitch this line
from the folded edge to the notch at
the side. Trim back the seam allowance
to ¼in (6mm) and clip at the notch to
release seam allowances; if the placket
has an angled top then miter off to the
point. NB: from here, this example
refers to a placket with a pointed end.

Turn out the placket, pull out the seam
allowance at the notch point, and press
the seam flat.

TIP

It may be necessary to fuse the
placket and underlap; this must
be decided before you start
construction.

④

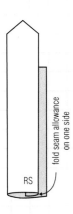

Fold and press the seam allowance to the wrong side of the placket.

⑤

UNDERLAP

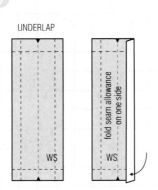

The underlap is the length of the slit plus seam allowances of ½in (1.5cm) at each end. The width should be 1¼in (3cm), which includes ¼in (6mm) seam allowance, giving a finished binding of ⅜in (1cm).

⑥

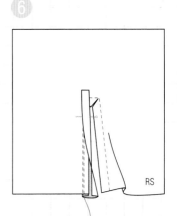

On the sleeve, reinforce the opening by staystitching ¼in (6mm) away from the marked slit all around. Cut up the slit to within ⅜in (1cm) of the top and then clip into the corners. At this point, decide the front and back edges of the opening; this will determine which side the placket is sewn upon. Align the RS of the unfolded seam allowance of the underlap to the WS back edge of the slit, and stitch. Press the seam allowances into the underlap, then fold the underlap toward the RS, encasing the raw edges. Pin the folded edge over to cover the first seam and edge-stitch through all the layers, stopping at the top corner.

⑦

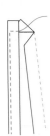

Fold the triangular section at the top of the slit and pin it to the underlap. Stitch together across the bottom of the triangle.

⑧

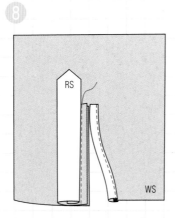

Align the RS of the unfolded placket edge to the WS of the front slit edge, pin, and stitch.

PATTERN DEVELOPMENT

Openings and fastenings

⑨

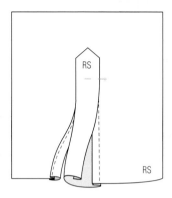

⑩

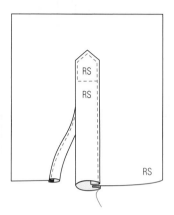

Press the seam allowances into the placket, trimming to reduce bulk if necessary. Turn the placket through to the RS, aligning the folded edge of the placket to the first stitch line. Pin or baste to keep in place.

Edgestitch through all the layers, from the cuff continuing up the side of the folded placket edge, pivoting around the point at the top of the placket, and finishing by sewing across the top of the slit (to reinforce), as shown.

1. Pin-tuck dress.

(Photo credit: Internacionale)

BOUND PLACKET

This method may be done with a binding attachment on your sewing machine. It is used mainly for dress shirts, where the cuffs are cuff-linked together, and for lightweight or sheer fabrics, as it gives a clean, "unworked" look that is extremely durable. As the edges overlap, it can be used with any lapped cuff.

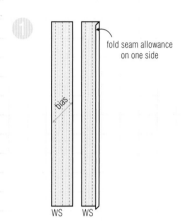

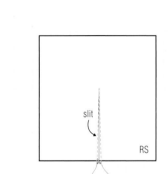

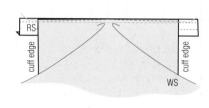

Cut a self-bias binding 1¼in (3cm) wide and twice the length of the marked slit. Press one side ¼in (6mm) under to the WS and mark a ¼in (6mm) seam along the other side.

Reinforce the placket by staystitching from the edge to the point, pivoting and stitching back to the edge. Slash to the point.

Open out the slit and pin the binding to the sleeve, right sides facing, with the unfolded edge aligned as shown. Stitch, and press seam allowances toward the binding.

TIP

For more accuracy, drop down to a lower stitch length when stitching up to corners.

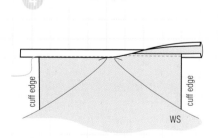

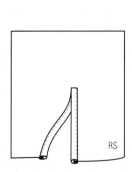

Fold the binding over to the WS, encasing the raw edges. Line up the folded edge with the stitching line, pin in place, and edgestitch.

The finished binding.

PATTERN DEVELOPMENT
Openings and fastenings

ONE-PIECE PLACKET BAND

This type of placket is suitable for either neck or sleeve openings.

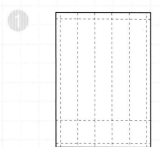

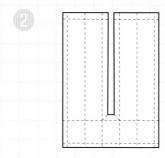

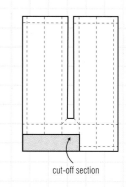

cut-off section

Draw a rectangle the length of the slit opening plus at least 1in (2.5cm) (this is for the overlap that reinforces the placket) and seam allowances (¼in/6mm). The width should be five times the required finished width of placket (determined by button size and design specifications) plus seam allowances (for the top edge, use the seam allowance used on the neckline on the body of the garment).

On the middle section of the placket, mark seam allowances for the opening.

The placket is drafted with one side longer than the other; this creates the overlap that in womenswear is on the right-hand side and in menswear on the left. The underlap side should be made ⅝in (1.5cm) shorter so that its raw edge is enclosed by the overlap. On the underlap side, square off a line ⅝in (1.5cm) up from the bottom to below the overlap seam and square down.

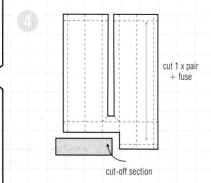

cut 1 x pair + fuse

cut-off section

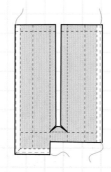

Remove this rectangle from the main section.

Apply interfacing (if necessary) to the wrong sides of the placket. Fold and press in seam allowances on the sides, and pin or baste at the bottom edge of the front band if necessary.

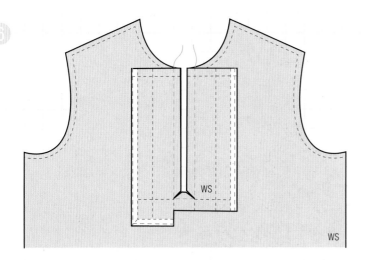

Pin the RS of the placket to the WS of the garment, aligning markings. Stitch along seam lines, pivoting at the corners.

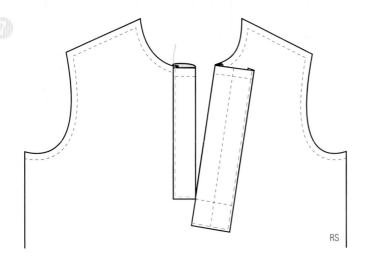

Snip into the corners and trim seam allowances if needed. Turn the placket through to the RS of the garment. Press the long seams inward toward the placket and press the triangular end down. Fold and press the shorter placket side along the fold line, positioning the edge over the original seam line, and pin. Edgestitch along the folded edge.

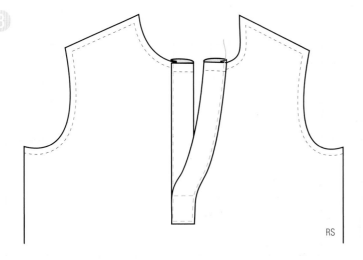

Fold and press the other (longer) side of the placket along the fold line, positioning the edge over the original seam line, and pin in place. Edgestitch along the folded edge, from top to bottom, and, pivoting on corners, carry on stitching as shown so that both placket sides are stitched together and all raw edges are enclosed.

PATTERN DEVELOPMENT
Openings and fastenings

FASTENINGS

Fastenings are more than just a functional detail to a garment, allowing garment openings to be securely closed. They can be used to enhance design and to attract focus to an area of the garment, as well as contrast visual styles.

ZIPPERS

Zippers are one of the most commonly used forms of garment fastening; they are strong and can be applied in many ways. Their most typical use is to join two parts, or sides of a garment, but they can also enable sections of a garment to be detachable, allowing multifunctional use. Because of the gradual method of opening/closing, zippers can both restrict and provide fullness to an area of a garment, which can be used to great effect.

Zippers can be included for visual purposes, and made to an array of designs, varying in length, the size and type of teeth (metal, plastic, coil), type and size of tape (nylon, cotton, coated), and the zipper pull (plastic, metal, rubber, leather). Zippers can have two sliders, which enable them to open from either end. There are five main types of zipper:

- **Plain:** A versatile zipper used for trouser flies and pocket openings, these are usually topstitched into position, leaving a visible line of stitching.

- **Invisible:** This is the least conspicuous of the zippers, giving the impression that it is just a seam. As the slider mechanism, tape, and teeth are hidden on the inside of the garment, only the pull is seen.

- **Separating:** This opens up completely and splits into two halves, and is ideal for openings on jackets, outerwear, and tops. It can be used for design purposes on garments, where a full opening is not essential but part of the look of the piece.

- **Invisible separating:** Sometimes known as bodice zippers, these also open up completely but give the look of an invisible zipper, which is inconspicuous when fastened.

- **Lightweight invisible:** This is a lighter-weight, gauzy tape that is more suitable for softer, thinner fabrics, where a conventional zipper would shadow through or distort the garment.

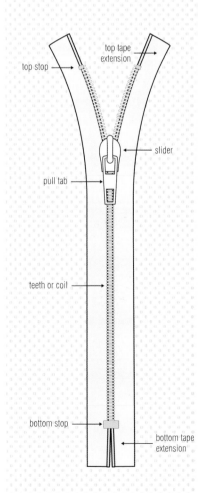

top tape extension

top stop

slider

pull tab

teeth or coil

bottom stop

bottom tape extension

OTHER TYPES OF FASTENINGS

The chosen method of closure depends on many factors, such as the type and look of garment, fabric weight, and the position of the fastening. The following are various common fastenings and their usage.

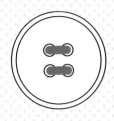

- **Buttons:** Please refer to the previous section. (1)

- **Snaps:** Also known as press studs and poppers, snaps have two interlocking parts, which click (or snap) together, and come apart when pulled. They can be either sewn on or riveted (for more heavy-duty garments), and can be used in conjunction with other fasteners such as a zipper. (2)

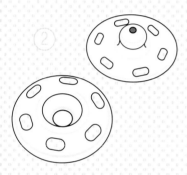

- **Hooks and eyes:** These sewn-on fastenings are formed of bent wire. They are composed of two parts: a hook, and a flat eyelet into which the hook fits when fastened. They are available in a range of sizes and finishes, including thread-covered (which can also be done by hand). Hooks and eyes are ideal for fabrics with a long pile, such as fur, which would trap within any other fastenings. They can be used as a fastening on their own (in a series of hooks and eyes) or with others, such as to ensure secure closure at the top of a zipper. (3)

VISIBLE ZIPPER

The visible zipper method needs a plain zipper, and can be used for decorative effect. This type of zipper can be inserted into a section of a garment without the need for a seam. This method can be adapted to create a letterbox-style visible zipper, suitable for pocket openings. The facing used to create the opening for the zipper can be attached to a lining or the edge finished off in another method, such as binding or overlocking.

MARKING ZIPPERS

Decide how much tape you want visible, allowing ¼in (6mm). Mark this either side of the length line, about ½in (1.2cm) up from the bottom edge, and mark a diagonal line into the corners. Create a rectangular facing from this pattern around 3–3½in (7.5–9cm), as shown. The facing will be cut in the self-fabric.

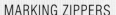

1

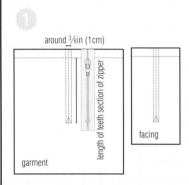

Mark the location and length of the opening on the pattern. The opening should be the length of the teeth of the zipper.

2

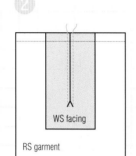

With right sides together, align garment body with facing at the opening. Pin and stitch around the opening, as shown, pivoting on corners Cut through the center of the opening from the seam allowance to the point of the triangular section, and clip diagonal lines into corners.

3

Turn through facing to wrong side of garment.

4

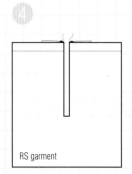

Press.

5

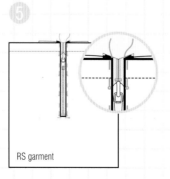

Place zipper behind facing, aligning teeth in the center of the opening, and pin.

6

Edgestitch zipper into position.

SEMI-CONCEALED ZIPPER

This method needs a plain zipper, and can be used for both closed and open-ended zip insertions.

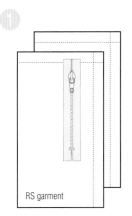

Draft seam allowances of ³⁄₈in (1cm) on both seam edges.

Place the zipper so that the top stopper aligns just below the stitch line, as shown. Mark with a pin the bottom of the lower metal stopper.

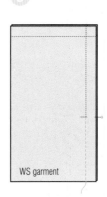

Stitch the seam, right sides together, up to this point.

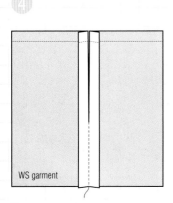

Press seam allowances open.

Place the zipper behind the opening, centering the zipper on the seam, and pin into position.

With a zipper foot, topstitch around the opening at approximately ³⁄₁₆–¹⁄₄in (4–6mm) out.

PATTERN DEVELOPMENT
Openings and fastenings

CONCEALED ZIPPER

This method uses a plain zipper. It is a suitable opening for skirts and pants.

Draft seam allowances of ⅜in (1cm) on both seam edges.

Place the zipper so that the top stopper aligns just below the stitch line, as shown. Mark with a pin the bottom of the lower metal stopper.

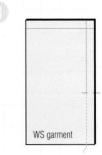

Stitch the seam, right sides together, up to this point.

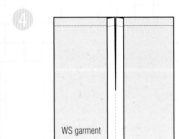

Press seam allowances open.

On the left-hand side, fold out seam allowance.

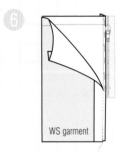

⅛–³⁄₁₆in (3–4mm) from seam, fold SA along opening, continuing for 2in (5cm) below end of zipper. Place zipper below, aligning fold ¹⁄₁₆in (2mm) away from teeth, and pin.

Open up zipper, and edgestitch using the zipper foot for the length of the zipper. To stitch past the zipper slider: with the needle down, lift the foot and pull the slider past, then continue sewing.

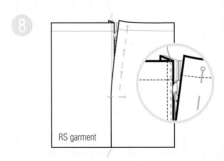

Pin the other side of the zipper to the right-hand side.

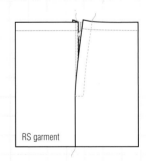

Topstitch into position with the zipper foot, following the edge of the zipper teeth, about ¹⁄₁₆in (2mm) out. Sewing toward the edge helps prevent a tuck forming at the bottom of the zipper.

INVISIBLE ZIPPER

This method is probably the most commonly used zipper type for dresses, skirts, and some tops. Buy invisible zippers slightly longer (½in/1.5cm) than the length required, as part of the length of the zipper is used when constructing.

RS garment

Draft ½in (1.5cm) seam allowances on both seam edges.

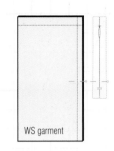

WS garment

At the bottom of the zipper, pin a point ½in (1.5cm) above the bottom stop, align the zipper as shown to the seam, and pin this point on the seam.

WS garment

Stitch the seam up to this point.

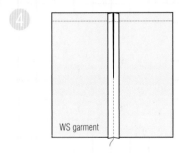

WS garment

Press seam allowances open.

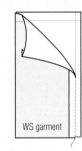

WS garment

Fold out seam allowances on one side.

WS garment

Align and pin the zipper to seam allowances. Open up the zipper and, using an invisible zipper foot, stitch the zipper to the seam allowance, opening out the zipper teeth as you go to ensure that the zipper is stitched closely. Stitch down the zipper to as far as the foot will allow.

WS garment

Repeat for the other side.

RS garment

Push the zipper pull through (there will be a small gap between the two sides at the bottom of the zip), and close the zipper. Press.

PATTERN DEVELOPMENT
Openings and fastenings

CHAPTER 12:
FINISHINGS, LININGS, AND FACINGS

HEMMING

Hems can be finished in a wide variety of ways; consider binding, perhaps in a lighter-weight fabric such as georgette. Alternatively, a raw or overlocked edge may be suitable for your specific design. A market-appropriate hem finish will give your garment a professional look. The most common hem finishes are listed below.

TURN AND OVERLOCK HEM

This is often the cheapest and quickest hem to turn, and is suitable for a wide variety of fabrics. Hem turn allowance can be adjusted as individual design dictates.

fold

Overlock edge.

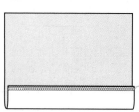

Fold hem allowance and stitch.

DOUBLE-TURN HEM

This is a self-neatening hem suitable for nonbulky fabrics, which can be sewn in conjunction with a topstitched or handstitched finish. Hem turn allowance can be adjusted as the individual design dictates.

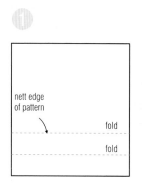

nett edge of pattern

fold

fold

Fold first turn allowance into position.

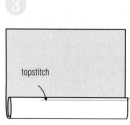

topstitch

Fold second turn allowance and topstitch: the raw edge is concealed in the double-turned fabric.

MACHINE-ROLLED HEM

A machine-rolled hem is a narrow, double-turned hem suitable for fine fabrics.

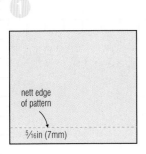

nett edge
of pattern

5⁄16in (7mm)

Select a suitable size stitch
in relation to fabric choice.

sew 1⁄8in (3mm)
from fabric edge

Roll the fabric against the first
line of stitching to create a very
narrow hem and sew a second
line of stitching.

Roll the fabric against the
second line of stitching and
complete hem with a third
line of stitching.

HEMMING STITCH

This is a handstitched hem finish that can be completed
with a double-turned or overlocked finish. Working from
right to left, bring the needle up through the hem edge.
Directly opposite and fractionally above the hem, take a
stitch, ensuring you catch only one or two threads of the
fabric, then move the needle diagonally through the hem
edge. Repeat for the length of the hem, spacing each
stitch roughly 1⁄4–3⁄8in (6–10mm) apart; do not draw the
thread tight as this will create a tension that will allow
stitch work to show from the right side.

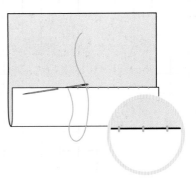

FACINGS

Facings are typically separate layers pattern-cut from the outer shell. They follow the same grain line as the outer and are usually cut in the self-fabric, though there are occasions where another material may be used—for both design and practical reasons. Facings have many purposes; they finish the edge of a garment as well as offering support to prevent distortion to profile edges. Because of the support they provide, facings are often interfaced, but it is important that the type of interfacing used is appropriate for both the fabric and the location. The facing should not be visible from the outside; therefore bulk (bulky fabric/interfacing) should be avoided.

Facings are often drafted $1/16$in (2mm) smaller on the profile edge; this allows for the seam to be hidden on the inside. Here, when attaching the facing, the outer shell's edge is traditionally rolled inward by $1/16$in (2mm). The seam is then edge-stitched on the facing side; the stitch holds it in position and prevents it from showing.

The unattached edge of the facing must itself be finished in a suitable way for the type of garment, such as by overlocking or binding. To ensure that the facing stays in position, the facing should be caught along its length by "invisibly" stitching (on the wrong side of the facing) onto the seam allowances that the panel intersects.

Facings can be used on their own or in conjunction with linings; the process to create the lining follows from those needed for the facing. This is covered in the next section.

COMMON AREAS FOR FACINGS

Common areas to face are the neckline, arm hole (which can be combined with the neckline), hem, waist, jacket revers, vents/slits, and garment openings. Facings are highly suitable for finishing shaped edges, such as a scalloped edge, where it would be near-impossible to finish with any other method.

1. Fearne Cotton midi-panel dress.

(Photo credit: Very)

BODICE FACING

This method creates separate facings for the neck and arm holes, and is suitable for tops and dresses.

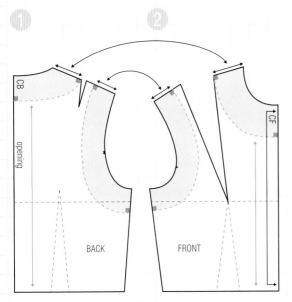

On the back bodice, mark points at regular intervals, at around 1½–2in (4–5cm) in from both the neckline and arm hole. Curve off the lines. To ensure a correct run, pattern pieces should be at right angles at the shoulder line, side seam, and CF (1).

Repeat for front, making sure that the measurements at shoulder lines and side seam match (2).

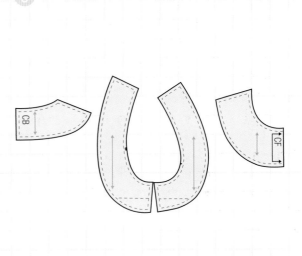

Trace off sections, adding seam allowances, pattern annotation, grainlines, and so on.

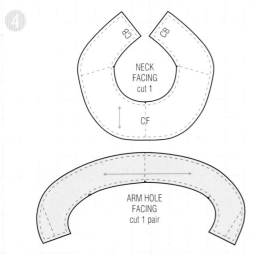

To simplify the facing pattern and eliminate the bulk of an extra shoulder seam, the front and back sections can be combined.

ALL-IN-ONE FACING

An all-in-one facing is one where the outer shell is extended to include the facing. As this requires a folded (rather than seamed) edge, this can only be done for areas with straight profile edges, such as the CF on a shirt or top. This example creates an all-in-one facing that allows for a CF button fastening.

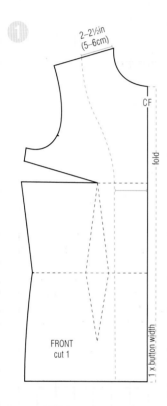

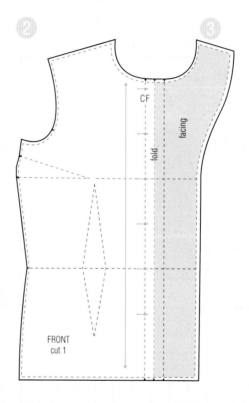

Decide on the size of the button. On the front bodice, draw a parallel line at a distance equal to the button diameter out from the CF; this will be the folded profile edge.

Draw a line from the bustline to the hem, parallel to the CF, about 2½–3in (6–7.5cm) in. Curve a line, as shown, from the bust to a point on the shoulder line around 2–2½in (5–6cm) down from the neck (2).

Mirror this facing section on the fold line (not the CF). Add seam allowances, notches, pattern annotation, and grainlines (3).

JACKET FACING

This method creates facings to finish the profile edges, as well as back facing to stabilize the back neck, where the collar attaches.

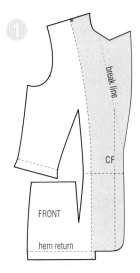

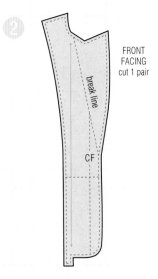

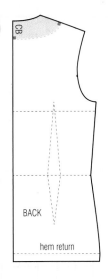

On the jacket front, mark a line parallel to the CF, around 2½–3in (6–7.5cm) in, from the hem to a point level with the break point, at the start of the break line. From here, curve a smooth line up to a point on the shoulder line around 2–2½in (5–6cm) down from the neck. The line should make a right angle at the shoulder line.

Trace a copy, adding seam allowances and pattern annotation.

On the jacket back, mark a point on the shoulder line around 2–2½in (5–6cm) down from the neck. Mark a point at the same measurement down from the neckline at the CB, and then at regular intervals down from the neckline. Connect these points and curve off the line, ensuring a right angle at CB and shoulder line.

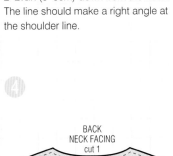

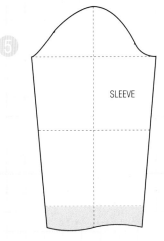

Mirror back pattern piece at CB. Add seam allowances, notches, pattern annotation, and grainlines to all pieces.

For the sleeve facing, mark a section around 1½–2in (4–5cm) up from the hem.

Trace a copy, adding seam allowances and pattern annotation.

PATTERN DEVELOPMENT
Finishings, linings, and facings

LININGS

Linings are an inner fabric shell, used on garments to hide the raw seam edges and internal structure (such as padding, interfacing, or pocket bags). They also prevent wear and strain on the main garment body. Linings are drafted from the main garment pattern, and are mostly used in conjunction with facings (see previous section). An extra allowance is made to the lining pattern at areas such as the CB, arm hole, and hem so that the lining does not distort the outer shell when worn.

When choosing a lining fabric, it is important to choose a material that can move and give with the wearer; those that are smooth or silky, in addition, enable the garment to be put on more easily over other clothing. Fabrics such as viscose and acetate are often used as they both drape well and do not insulate body heat.

Some linings, such as on a traditional jacket, fully conceal the garment inner, whereas others may only be partially lined. A summer-weight jacket, for instance, could be lined solely on the fronts and the upper back, and with or without sleeve lining, so that interfacing and shoulder pads are hidden.

Linings do not always completely bag out the garment; a skirt or dress may be hemmed and left to hang separately (the lining hem overlapping the main garment hem). The lining is then held in position with chainstitch loops.

CONSTRUCTING A LINED GARMENT

In a lined garment, the lining and outer are constructed separately, and then attached (bagged out) to each other by stitching around the garment profile edges.

1. Holly Willoughby crochet-collar tea dress.

(Photo credit: Very)

BASIC BODICE LINING WITH FRONT OPENING

① 1

Follow steps as for front and back bodice facings. Mark extra notches as shown. Draw desired width of hem facing, approx. 1½–2in (4–5cm).

② 2

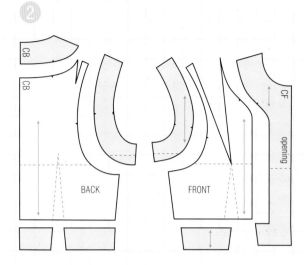

Subtract facings from main body sections.

③ 3

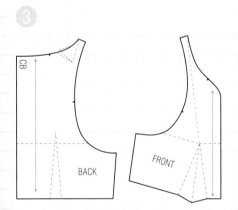

Pivot back shoulder dart into neckline; smooth curve at seam, leaving in dart amount as ease. Pivot front shoulder dart into waistline.

A small bust pleat to add room and comfort can be put at this stage into the front arm hole at a point below the front balance notch by pivoting part (1in/2.5cm) of the shoulder dart and the remainder into the waist.

④ 4

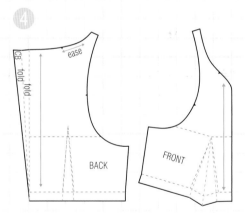

At the bottom edge of the lining, add hem return of 1in (2.5cm). This creates a small pleat at the bottom of the lining. Redraw darts to the new edge, but keeping the original dart width. Add a box pleat at the back by adding 1½in (4cm) and tapering it down to the waist.

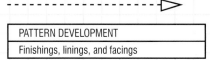

PATTERN DEVELOPMENT
Finishings, linings, and facings

⑤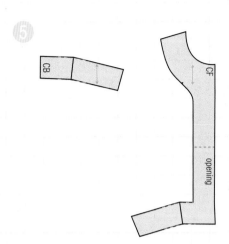

Combine facing pieces for front and back as shown;
curve off angles where pieces join.

⑥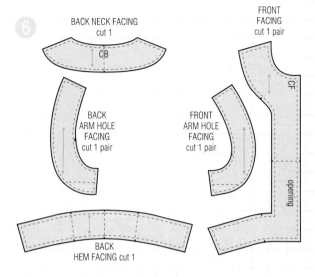

BACK NECK FACING
cut 1

CB

FRONT
FACING
cut 1 pair

CF

BACK
ARM HOLE
FACING
cut 1 pair

FRONT
ARM HOLE
FACING
cut 1 pair

opening

BACK
HEM FACING cut 1

Mirror facings at CB. Add seam allowances, notches,
and pattern annotation.

⑦

Add seam allowances and pattern annotation.

REDUCING BULK

When using thick fabrics,
or widely spaced topstitching,
it will be necessary to miter
the corners of the pocket prior
to bagging out.

SKIRT LINING

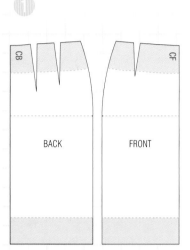

Mark waistband facings on skirt.

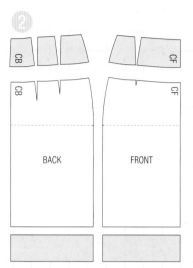

Subtract facing sections from body of skirt to make lining.

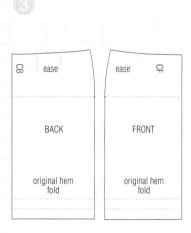

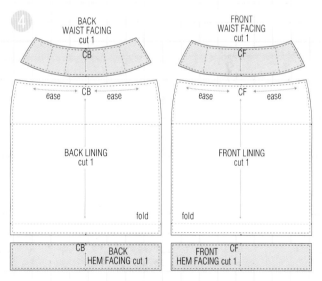

Curve off top edge of lining, leaving in darts as ease.
If the remaining dart is more than ½in (1.2cm), half of the
dart amount should be taken off the side seam, tapering
to nothing at the hip (use the block to trace a new hip curve).
Add an amount (1in/2.5cm) at the bottom edge to overlap the
hem facing. Add the same amount again to create a hem return.

Mirror pattern pieces at CF and CB. Add seam allowances,
notches, and pattern annotation. Note how the front and back
waist facings are created by closing the waist darts and smoothing
the joins.

JACKET LINING

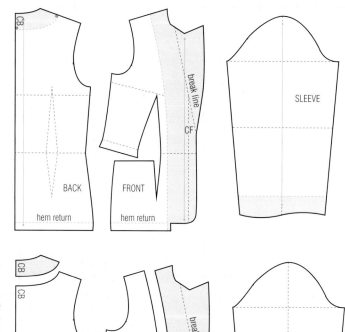

Follow steps as for front and back jacket facings.

BACK

FRONT

hem return

hem return

SLEEVE

Take away facing sections from main body.

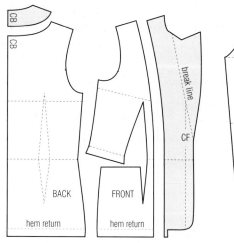

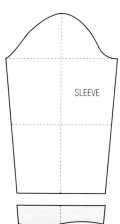

CB

CB

break line

CF

SLEEVE

BACK

FRONT

hem return

hem return

Mark a point ³⁄₁₆in (4mm) up from front and back shoulder line at arm hole; redraw new shoulder line, tapering to facing and new arm hole, tapering to balance point. At underarm point on side seam, mark a point ⁵⁄₈in (1.5cm) up and ³⁄₁₆in (4mm) out; redraw new arm hole tapering to balance, and new side seam tapering to waist.

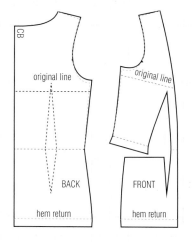

CB

original line

original line

BACK

FRONT

hem return

hem return

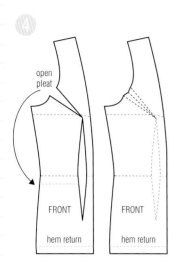

Close dart at waist, opening to create pleat at arm hole.

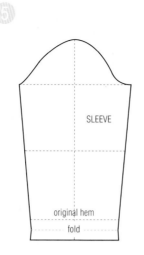

Create a pleat at the bottom of the sleeve lining by adding 1in (2.5cm) for the overlap of the sleeve hem facing and another 1in (2.5cm) for the hem lining return.

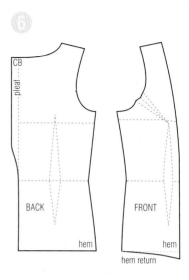

Remove hem return at back lining. On the front lining, curve a line up from the front edge at the hem return up to the side seam on the hemline. At CB add 1in (2.5cm), squaring down from the neck, and then tapering to the waist as shown. When sewn, this will create a pleat to add room for movement across the shoulders.

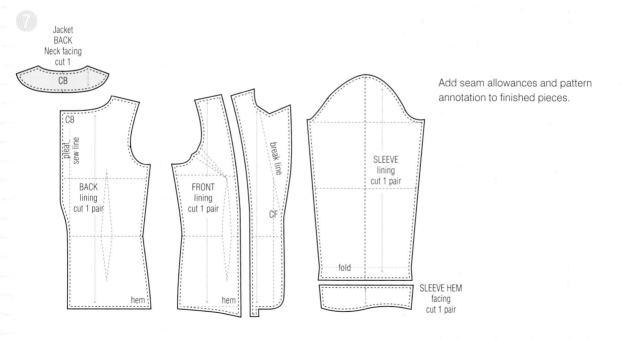

Add seam allowances and pattern annotation to finished pieces.

PATTERN DEVELOPMENT
Finishings, linings, and facings

CHAPTER 13: POCKETS

Pockets can be functional, decorative, or both. They can be applied or inserted into a garment, as in the case of a patch pocket, or form a structural element, such as the jean-style pocket described below. Pockets can be cut to match or contrast with the grain of the garment.

Ensure that pockets are positioned and sized to be flattering on the final garment. You will notice that pockets are not always positioned on a true horizontal or vertical line, but are often angled to be more flattering. The chest welt pocket on a traditional man's suit is a good example of this: the pocket is angled slightly upward, although it appears almost straight as it molds around the body profile. Applied or inserted pockets such as a patch can be added to a toile after the first fitting, once their position is ascertained in relation to the completed garment.

PATCH POCKETS

Patch pockets can come in any shape or size. The top of the pocket will require a turn-back (or hem) at the open edge of the pocket to provide stability and ensure the wrong side of the fabric does not show; in the case of a pocket with a shaped opening edge, a facing will be required.

UNLINED PATCH POCKET

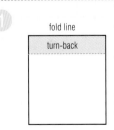

Plan the pocket and turn-back, and mark the position of the pocket on the main pattern piece with drill holes.

Add turn-back onto patch pocket, add seam allowances, and mark fold line with a notch.

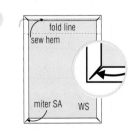

Press seam allowances to wrong side and miter corners. Sew turn-back hem.

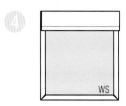

Lightly press the turn-back.

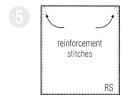

reinforcement
stitches

RS

Sew to main garment, using backstitching or a more decorative stitch
to reinforce the pocket opening.

LINED PATCH POCKET

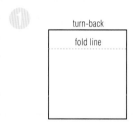

turn-back

fold line

Plan the pocket and turn-back, and
mark the position of the pocket on the
main pattern piece with drill holes.

POCKET LINING
cut 1 x lining

The lining is the pocket minus
turn-back. Add seam allowances.

turn-back

fold line

cut 1 x self

The pocket piece is the pocket
dimensions plus turn-back. Add seam
allowances and mark the fold line with
a notch.

lining WS

RS

Attach lining and pocket pieces
and press open seam allowances.

lining WS

Sew around the pocket, leaving an
opening to bag pieces out. Sew to
garment as for patch pocket.

PATTERN DEVELOPMENT
Pockets

CURVED PATCH POCKETS

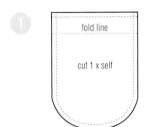

Plan pocket as for unlined patch pocket.

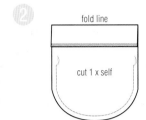

Fold and neaten the pocket facing. Loosen the upper tension on your machine and sew around the curve, leaving long threads to gauge the curve in the next step.

Pull bobbin thread tight, encouraging the SA to turn. Use a nett copy of the pocket as a pressing template and flatten the SA. Return tension to your usual setting and continue construction as for patch pocket.

PATCH POCKET WITH FLAP

Plan the pocket flap, extending the flap beyond the width of the patch pocket to ensure the flap covers the uppermost construction of the patch pocket.

Add ⅜in (1cm) seam allowance to pattern piece and label as pocket flap lining.

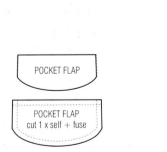

Make another copy of the pocket flap and add ⅛in (3mm) to the outer edge. Now add ⅜in (1cm) seam allowance to the pattern piece and label as pocket flap.

Bag out the pocket flap and complete with topstitching if necessary. Neaten the open edge of the pocket flap and secure to garment.

1. A patch pocket has been used in combination with a contrasting fabric to great effect in this dress.

(Photo credit: Internacionale)

POCKET IN SIDE SEAM

In its most simple form, a pocket bag is simply set in to the side seam and is cut in one piece with your garment. To reduce bulk or to minimize fabric costs, the pocket bag can be cut separately in lining or contrast fabric and the seam allowances offset to ensure the pocket seam does not show at the side seam. A strip of interfacing, or cotton tape, is positioned at the pocket opening to ensure that it does not stretch and sag during use.

SET-IN POCKET IN SEAM

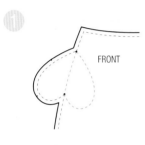

Plan pocket and set in to front garment pattern piece.

Mirror pocket addition onto back pattern piece.

Sew side seam as one. For an open seam, miter pocket pieces on front only or overlock front and back in one.

POCKET IN SEAM WITH SEPARATE POCKET BAG

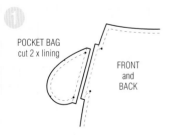

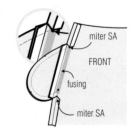

Divide the pocket bag from the main pattern, setting the pocket seam back from the side seam to reduce unnecessary bulk.

With RS together, sew a pocket bag to front and back pattern pieces.

Sew side seam as one and miter pocket pieces on front only, to press SA open or overlock front and back separately prior to joining side seam.

PATTERN DEVELOPMENT
Pockets

FRONT POCKETS

CURVED JEAN-STYLE FRONT POCKET

This pocket forms a structural element of the finished garment. Plan the pocket opening and the pocket bag, tracing off pieces as shown in the diagram. Note that the front side hip has a large seam allowance at its bottom edge to ensure that it is hidden by the pocket facing.

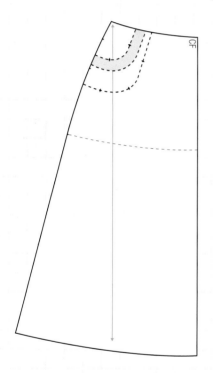

FRONT SIDE
HIP
cut 1 x self

POCKET
FUSING
cut 1 x fuse

HIP SECTION
cut 1 x lining

POCKET
FACING
cut 1 x lining

Overlock the edge of the front side hip and sew on top of hip section.

With right sides together, sew pocket facing to skirt.

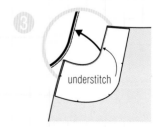

understitch

Turn pocket facing to WS and understitch SA to pocket facing.

Fuse pocket opening on WS of skirt.

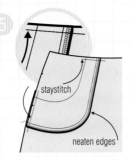

Sew the hip section and pocket facing. Stitch the pocket opening.

Join side seams as usual, with right sides together.

TWO-PIECE WELT POCKET

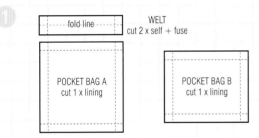

Plan welt size. Draft welt pattern to 4 x welt width and add SA to outermost edges only. Mark fold with a notch. Plan the pocket bag depth. Draft pocket bag B to these measurements. Draft pocket bag A to same width plus welt pattern in length.

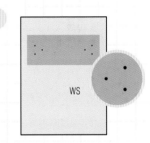

Interface WS of fabric and mark welt opening with drill holes. Note that the innermost mark is ³⁄₈in (1cm) from outer edge.

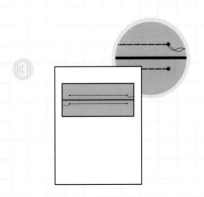

Lay welts onto main fabric with WS together and sew in line with drill holes.

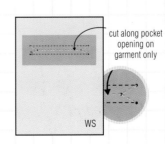

Turn work over to WS and cut pocket opening on garment only, then miter corners.

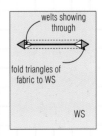

Fold along stitch line and post welts through pocket opening. Fold mitered triangles to WS.

PATTERN DEVELOPMENT
Pockets

⑥

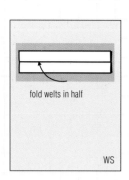

fold welts in half

WS

Fold welts in half and lightly press. The welts can be tacked together at fold to stabilize during rest of construction.

⑦

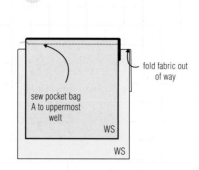

fold fabric out of way

sew pocket bag A to uppermost welt

WS

WS

Sew pocket bag A to uppermost welt along the stitch line created in stage 3.

⑧

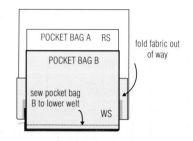

POCKET BAG A   RS

POCKET BAG B

fold fabric out of way

sew pocket bag B to lower welt

WS

Sew pocket bag B to lower welt along the stitch line created in stage 3.

⑨

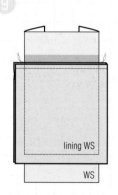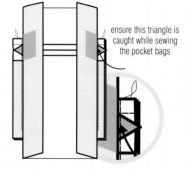

ensure this triangle is caught while sewing the pocket bags

lining WS

WS

Sew pocket bags together, ensuring that the mitered triangles are caught; neaten edges of pocket bag if required.

⑩

RS

Finished pocket from right side.

WELT POCKET WITH FLAP

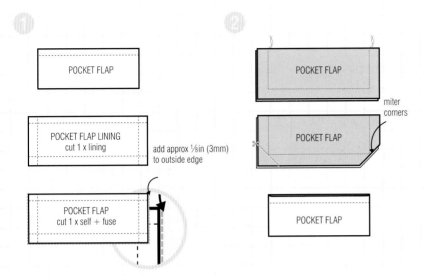

1 Draft flap pattern. Add 1 x welt width to top edge and ³⁄₈in (1cm) to sides and lower edge. Make another copy. Add ¹⁄₈in (3mm) to edge of one piece to allow for fabric loss while bagging out.

2 With RS together, sew pocket flap and pocket flap lining together, leaving one side open. Miter corners and bag out. Topstitch if required.

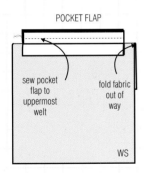

3 The pocket flap is posted through pocket opening and the pocket bag is attached to welt and flap in one, as at stage 7 of welt construction.

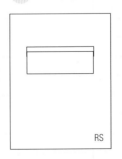

4 Finished pocket from right side.

DRAFTING A FLAP ON THE FOLD

The flap can also be drafted on the fold and cut in 1 x self + interfacing. Cutting the flap on the fold reduces bulk and offers the opportunity to use a contrast fabric if desired.

1. Jacket with two-piece welt pocket.

(Photo credit: La Redoute)

PATTERN DEVELOPMENT
Pockets

ONE-PIECE WELT POCKET

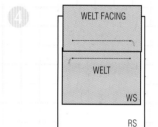

Plan welt size. Draft welt piece at 2 x welt width and welt facing pattern to 1 x welt width plus ⅝in (1.5cm) to length. Add ⅝in (1.5cm) SA all around.

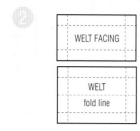

Plan pocket bag depth. Draft pocket bag to these measurements. Add ⅝in (1.5cm) SA and cut 2 x lining.

Interface WS of fabric and mark welt opening with drill holes. Note innermost drill hole is ⅝in (1.5cm) from outer edge.

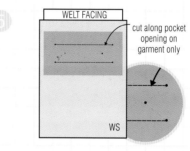

Lay welts onto main fabric with WS together and sew in line with drill holes.

Turn work over to WS and cut pocket opening on garment only, then miter corners.

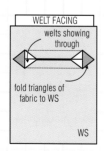

Fold along stitch line and post welts through pocket opening. Fold mitered triangles to WS.

1. Selma tunic dress with one-piece welt pocket.

(Photo credit: Want Her Dress)

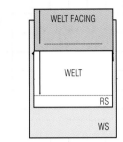

Temporarily fold welt facing upward and fold welt downward, ready to attach the pocket bags.

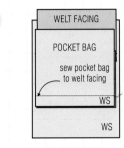

With right sides together, sew one pocket bag to welt as shown in the diagram.

Fold welt in half and drop pocket bag into position, noting that the SA is facing toward the garment. Press SA open.

With RS together, sew the second pocket bag piece to welt facing.

Drop welt facing into position and press SA open. Sew pocket bags as for welt, if required, and neaten pocket bag as one.

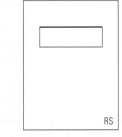

Finished pocket from right side.

NOTE:

Note that the extra height added to the welt facing in stage 2 has enabled the SA to be offset, thus reducing unnecessary bulk.

4

THE DESIGNER MAKER

CHAPTER 14: GOING PRO

Transforming a hobby into a business can be a big step; many people who work in this field have undertaken formal training or worked in an existing fashion company to learn the ins and outs of the business. However, many successful businesspeople can grow an enterprise from a passion or enthusiasm for their chosen field.

It is essential that you thoroughly research your market and ensure that you have a clear idea of your potential customer. Do you have a unique vision of your brand and the types of garments you wish to produce? Are you going to sell directly or via independent boutiques? Perhaps you also want to offer accessories such as scarves, belts, or bags; these can offer an entry-level purchase, allowing your customer to buy into your brand at minimal cost.

You may need to start off performing every role, such as sourcing, design, construction, and marketing. Spend your time wisely on the things that you do well, or where your time is put to best use. As your business grows, it is likely that you will need to outsource some elements of the collection. This will enable you to focus on other aspects, such as research (fabrics, trims, design development), merchandising and promoting the collection, as well as working with buyers. It can take time to build a successful brand; a good first step can be to work to commission or test the market with a small online store.

ALEXANDRA KING

Gain as much experience as possible. Don't ever cut corners when it comes to the product. Don't over-indulge in equipment or fabrics, and believe in yourself, your value, and your product. Be prepared for a lot of hard work, too.

Feral Childe is a US-based womenswear line by bi-coastal design duo Moriah Carlson (Brooklyn, NY) and Alice Wu (Oakland, CA): www.feralchilde.com

Alexandra King is an independent bridal and womenswear label handmade in the UK: www.alexandra-king.com

1. Scroll tee and pleated skirt by Feral Childe.

(Photo credit: Feral Childe)

FERAL CHILDE

Start locally! Know your customer. Learn how to sell. Keep that day job for as long as you can and work for other fashion companies, both big and small. If you work for a small company you'll see what it's going to be like running your own company.

DESIGN DEVELOPMENT

Collections are usually divided into seasons: spring/summer and fall/winter, with other smaller releases such as a resort or pre-collection bridging the main collections. Large main collections can be further divided into launches, with individual themes and color palettes, that will enter the market at different stages. This cycle may or may not be appropriate to your business model.

In the industry, the design cycle often begins with fabric and trim sourcing. Fabrics, trims, and fastenings can be sourced in many ways. To get the best deal, especially if bigger quantities are wanted, go straight to the supplier or wholesaler rather than buying through a retailer. Note, however, that most of these companies have a minimum order, which may be prohibitive. It is important that you select materials and trims that reflect not only your spending power but also have working properties that are appropriate to the intended garments contained within your range.

When beginning a new collection, gather together concepts and design details that excite and inspire you as a designer. Sources of inspiration can come from everywhere and anywhere. It is important to keep your mind open; quite often ideas come from completely diverse places to create exciting and new contrasts.

FERAL CHILDE

We often begin with very abstract ideas—loosely connected themes not directly related to fashion or clothing at all.

SKETCHBOOKS AND MOOD BOARDS

Sketchbooks are not only the best place to keep ideas and store photographs and clippings, they're also perfect for recording technical notes and sketches to ensure you fully develop design ideas. Do not be put off if you feel you do not draw particularly well or are rusty: practice will make it easier for you to convey your ideas in this format, and observations from life or photography will improve your 3D "vocabulary." Experiment with different media such as collage, watercolors, or marker pens to communicate your ideas. A fashion croquis can be invaluable for getting your initial ideas down quickly.

1. A sketchbook page with ideas for accessories.

(Photo credit: Feral Childe)

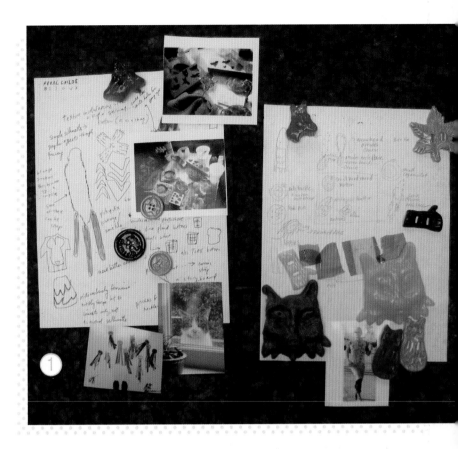

FERAL CHILDE

We try to use the most sustainable materials we can find. This means natural fibers from silks to organic cotton, linen, Tencel, and hemp blends. Another option is to use vintage deadstock or surplus fabrics left over from other manufacturers. Sometimes we'll use these fabrics as is, but we have also given them new life by overdyeing or overprinting.

Mood boards can be a more focused version of the sketchbook and are a great way of communicating the feel of a collection. Find a format that works best for you, whether this is on presentation boards, large polystyrene pinboards, a CAD presentation, or even a video mood board.

The Autumnal
Travelling Tinker
Autumn/Winter 2012

1

1. An example of a designer's mood board.

(Photo credit: Katie Mills)

FERAL CHILDE

About 70 percent of the collection is built from past patterns because we always offer a certain number of variations on past bestsellers/ staples. We update and improve the fit of these and reinterpret them in different fabrics, which requires us to adapt the pattern.

BUILDING A COLLECTION

Key to a successful, cohesive collection is good design development. It is important to remember that the design process does not end with an illustration of your proposed design but also includes the thorough investigation of each garment in terms of silhouette, proportion, and detailing. Before settling on your final idea, sketch it out multiple times, playing with design details such as pocket placement, topstitching, or finishing methods. Constantly ask yourself questions. How does one get into the garment? Is that the best length for the skirt or bodice? Would this particular garment look better with a large full sleeve or one that is closer-fitting? Each design decision has repercussions on the pattern drafting and construction processes; thorough attention to design development ensures that you are planning ahead and have a good working drawing of a garment that is actually achievable.

Your business model may entail the creation of "one-off" garments or the cyclic production of a collection of garments. When creating multiple items within one release, range planning becomes key. It is important that you begin to think in terms of a capsule collection, ensuring that pieces interact as a whole. Repeating design features across different garments within your range can help to build a cohesive look. The fashion industry appears to be focused on constant reinvention and pressure to keep reinventing the wheel, but do not be distracted by this. Styles from previous seasons can be updated with new design details and used as a basis for new garments within your next collection.

PRICING YOUR PRODUCT

A small fashion producer will find it very difficult to compete with prices in the mass market; you need to offer your clients something different and of a sufficiently good quality to justify the prices you will need to set as an independent designer.

The design process not only includes the themes and ideas behind your collection but also entails keeping tight control over the total cost of your final product. Ensure you keep an eye on the running cost of your business, including materials, manufacturing costs, machinery, and utilities before you even start to turn a profit and pay yourself for your services. You may find you need to make compromises as you go along, and it is important you do not overspend, thus pricing yourself out of the market.

TECHNICAL CONSIDERATIONS

To be able to outsource elements of a collection, such as print and embroidery, or the pattern cutting and construction of the garment as a whole, the most vital thing is good communication. For the factories or outsourced freelancers who are involved in garment drafting and production, a clear technical drawing and specification sheet for each garment is imperative. The sewing contractor must be able to understand each detail so a successful interpretation of the garment can be made.

TECHNICAL DRAWING

Technical drawings are a precise and proportional rendering of your design; illustrative devices such as the stylistic lengthening of the figure, which often occurs in a fashion sketch, are not used. This type of drawing is often referred to as a "flat," which indicates that the garment is drawn as it appears laid flat. It is essential that both front and back views are included; some designs may also warrant a side view. The flat should also include any details such as topstitching, button placement, and seam construction, alongside some basic working measurements such as neckline drops, skirt/bodice lengths, and opening positions. A well-annotated technical drawing serves as a reference throughout the drafting and manufacturing process.

ALEXANDRA KING

I made lots of mistakes when starting out; mainly this was due to undervaluing myself, as many creatives do. It can be terrifying trying to sell your personal work, but when you have your product perfected it's easy to stand by it and believe in yourself.

SPECIFICATION SHEETS

A specification sheet also contains a technical drawing and is a standardized guide for quality control both in-house and throughout the manufacturing chain. It exhibits more detailed finishing details and contains a column for precise measurements of both pattern and garment. The final column shows the "tolerance," or acceptable margin of difference, between the two.

A specification sheet will include the following information, as relevant to the individual design:

- Lengths of important parts of the garment, such as openings, cuff/waistband widths, collar size, hem length, and details such as pockets and flaps.

- Type and code of fastening, with exact details of color and finish.

- Codes and color of fabric, and where they are used.

- Topstitching, thread color, size of stitch, and distance from seam (e.g., 1/4 stitch).

- Codes and color of trimmings, such as drawstrings, ribbon, or eyelets.

- Any embroidery or print placements.

- Costing and consumption information.

The example specification sheet shown here contains the minimum information that should be logged for each garment. In industry this document may be referred to as a Specification or Technical Pack and will also include detail such as labeling and grading information.

SEASON/DATE:

Style Ref:
Description:

FABRIC/TRIM:

Self/Main:
Contrast:
Lining:

COLOUR:

SKETCH AND MEASUREMENT POSITIONS:

MEASUREMENT POSITIONS	PATTERN	GARMENT	TOLERANCE
a	front length: SNP to hem—in a waisted style ensure you specify to waist seam or hem			
b	back length: CB to hem, CB to waist etc.			
c	neckline straight: SNP to SNP			
d	front neckline drop			
e	back neckline drop			
f	shoulder			
g	across back 1/2—usually measured 4³/₄in (12cm) down from CB neckline but ensure you specify			
h	arm hole 1/2—if garment has a sleeve this can be measured straight, no sleeve measure along curve			
i	across bust 1/2—usually measured 1in (2.5cm) down from underarm seam but ensure this is specified			
j	waist 1/2—specify distance from underarm			
k	hem 1/2 straight—a flared hem should be laid flat to record this measurement			
l	hem dip—specify CF or CB			
m	side seam—in a waisted style ensure you specify to/from waist seam etc.			
n	overarm sleeve length			
o	underarm sleeve length			
p	bicep 1/2—usually 1in (2.5cm) from underarm seam but ensure you specify			
q	elbow 1/2—fold sleeve so hem touches underarm seam and measure the sleeve across the fold			
r	cuff 1/2			
s	cuff width			
t	waist seam to pocket			
u	pocket position: specify position from nearest seams			
v	pocket depth			
w	pocket width			

THE DESIGNER MAKER

Going pro

PROMOTING YOUR WORK

Branding, marketing, and merchandising are central when building
a collection. They encompass everything including the logo, packaging,
and hangtags, to convey a cohesive look and message to the consumer.
Marketing is the method by which you present the collection: advertising,
an online presence such as a website or a blog, catwalk presentations, or trunk
shows. Lookbooks are a selling and promotional tool that can be as creative
as you like and can sell the story of your collection. Your mood board and/or
selected pages from your sketchbook can be collated to form the backbone
of this type of presentation. Line sheets are slightly more staid and contain
technical drawings, fabric, color, and pricing information; it is these, as well
as a sample garment, that potential buyers from retail outlets will be most
interested in.

Social media and the Internet enable you to interact directly with potential
customers and can help to create a buzz around your collection and product.
This method is increasingly harnessed by big brands and smaller independent
designers alike. A blog or picture-hosting website can be an excellent way to
begin building your brand identity without the expense of website design and
hosting. It is best to post regularly rather than sporadically, as this will keep
your readers' interest up. Consider posting sneak peeks of your workspace or
imagery and music or design that inspires you. Tagging uploaded content with
appropriate words to describe content as well as your name will start to move
you up the search-engine listings. The use of analytic tools can allow you to
gain a good understanding of your market and the search terms by which
traffic is being directed to your site.

ALEXANDRA KING

I present the collections online in lots of detail along with a buildup
to the launch with all of our development images and inspirations.

1

FERAL CHILDE

We photograph the collections
and harness social media to
continue our outreach to stores
and customers.

E-TAILING

Electronic retailing, or e-tailing, is the term coined to describe the buying and
selling of retail goods via the Internet. This type of retailing can be particularly
suitable as a first step for your fashion entrepreneurship, benefiting from zero
or minimal setup costs compared to those of a physical retail space. Many
e-commerce sites have formed a partnership with PayPal, enabling the secure
sale of goods to anyone with an email address without the need for a credit card.

You may choose to set up your own standalone website to retail your goods,
but there is also a wide variety of e-commerce marketplaces such as Etsy,
which allow for personal storefronts among peer retailers. A potential e-tail
customer may hold a natural apprehension regarding sizing, which can be
overcome by providing some of the collated information from a specification
sheet for comparison against personal measurements.

THE DESIGNER MAKER

Going pro

GLOSSARY

bagging-out: to stitch two sections together, sewing around profile edges with right sides together. With one part left open, the section is then turned through, or "bagged out," enclosing all seams. Sections that are typically bagged out are collars and linings.

bias: a grain with natural stretch that runs diagonally at 45 degrees to the selvage.

balance: the proper "hang" or "fall" of a garment.

balance points: similar to notches, but used on a nett pattern for measuring pieces together and checking balance (e.g., sleeve pitch).

bishop sleeve: a sleeve that is fitted at the top and gathered into the cuff, using flare to make the extra fullness at the cuff.

break line: the line at which the rever naturally folds back.

break point: the point at which the rever starts to fold back to form the lapel.

cap sleeve: a very short sleeve. Can be drafted by slightly extending the shoulder line, so that it "caps" the shoulder, or can be set-in.

close a dart: to remove a dart so that it can be transferred, or "opened" in another position.

collar point: the pointed end of the collar where the lead edge and leaf edge meet.

construction lines: lines on the pattern giving specific information, e.g., dart position.

cut 1 pair: cut one plus a mirrored opposite.

cut 2: cut two identical pieces.

cut to fold/cut on fold: creates a mirrored piece from a half-section. This method is not used in mass industry. Fold a section of fabric and place fold line on pattern to fold.

darts: a form of suppression found, for example, around the bust, waist, and hips. These are stitched sections, usually triangular or diamond-shaped, that take in areas of excess fabric as shaping.

dolman: a set-in sleeve that has a dropped arm hole, but plenty of "lift" due to extra fabric being added at the underarm.

drafting: the creation of a basic sloper or block.

drape: the amount of extra fabric at the underarm, which allows the sleeve to be lifted comfortably. Common in dolman and kimono sleeves.

ease: an amount of fullness given to a garment to achieve a more comfortable fit. With seams that have been "eased in," the excess should be invisible and not gathered.

edgestitching: topstitching sewn closely (i.e., ⅛in/ 3mm) to the edge of the seam, or garment profile.

fall: the part of the collar that "falls" over, between the roll line and style line.

flat collar: a collar that sits flat around the shoulders.

fullness: extra fabric added to a pattern piece for shaping that can be used as flare, gather, or ease.

graded nest: a visual "stack" containing each size grade of a pattern piece, from smallest to largest.

grading: the practice of sizing a pattern piece up or down using set incremental grade rules, or measurements.

grain: the thread direction of the fabric. Although it can refer to either warp or weft, the term "grain" is commonly used in connection with the warp.

grainline: a straight line on the pattern piece that denotes the direction in which the pattern should lay, parallel to the warp.

increment: the specific amount in which size groups differ; to incrementally enlarge or decrease the pattern size.

interfacing: a textile used to stabilize another fabric. These can be either fusible or sewn-in, and are available in numerous weights and qualities.

lapel: the part of a rever that folds back over the break line and lays flat on the front.

lead edge: the front edge of a collar, e.g., the edges on a shirt collar between which the tie would sit.

leaf edge/style line: the outer edge of the collar.

leg-of-mutton: a very full sleeve, gathered into the arm hole, and gathered in at the elbow. The sleeve is then closely fitted from the elbow to the wrist. Common in Victorian times.

lift: the amount a sleeve can be moved comfortably when the arm is raised, without distorting the garment.

lining: an inner shell of the garment, made of a lighter-weight fabric, that encloses all the internal seams.

mirrored piece: a symmetrical pattern piece, which, flipped on a mirror line, creates the complete garment section.

miter: to cut away bulk from seam allowances at corners diagonally, so that they can be turned through fully, ensuring a sharp profile edge.

muslin: a test version of a garment, normally made in cotton fabric.

nett: a piece or section of pattern without seam allowance.

nett pattern: a pattern without seam allowance.

notches: small snips made in the seam allowance to mark where two garment pieces are to be matched and sewn together.

profile: the outer edge of a garment or garment section.

quarter-stitch: topstitching $\frac{1}{4}$ in (6mm) in from the profile edge. Seen on shirt collars and cuffs.

raglan: a sleeve that has the shoulder sections of the back and front bodice all in one, so that the sleeve extends up to the neck.

rever: a collar that is partially grown on to the front, and forms a permanent fold-back, as on a man's tailored jacket.

roll: a small amount of extra fabric given to allow a seam to be "rolled" so that the seam edge is hidden. Found, for example, on collars and revers.

run: the edge created when two pattern pieces join, such as the underarm, or the crutch. This line should "run" smoothly, rather than bump.

seam allowance (SA): an extra amount (for example ½in/1.5cm) added around the pattern to allow for garment pieces to be seamed together.

self/main: the main fabric of the garment.

selvage: the self-finished edges of the fabric. Derived from "self-edge."

set-in sleeve: a sleeve that is sewn in to a completely made-up arm hole, i.e. the shoulder and side seams are sewn before the sleeve is sewn in.

sink-stitch: to stitch "invisibly" into, or through, one seam, to attach another garment part underneath, such as a waistband facing. Also known as stab-stitching.

size chart: a standardized guide of body measurements for each size grade.

sleevehead: the (usually curved) section at the top of a sleeve, which is sewn into the arm hole.

sleeve pitch: the correct "hang" of the sleeve. Balance points, and accurate cutting, will control this.

sloper or block: a basic pattern that can be used as a starting point for drafting many styles of garment.

square-off: to mark a line at a right angles (90 degrees) to another.

stand: the part of the collar that stands up around the neck. Usually separate, e.g., on shirt collars. It can also be concealed.

suppression: shaping such as darts, tucks, or gathers, which take in excess fabric.

topstitch: a line of stitching that is seen on the right side of the fabric, sewn usually in a larger stitch length with topstitching thread. Topstitching can be both functional (adding strength to seams) and decorative.

twin-needle stitching: two, typically parallel, rows of stitching. Found, for example, on jeans pockets.

warp: the lengthwise yarns of the fabric, which run parallel to the edge.

weft: yarns that run across the fabric, at right angles to the edge.

wrap: the extra fabric added onto a collar and center front to enable the fronts to overlap and fasten up.

RESOURCES

USEFUL SOFTWARE

Fittingly Sew
PC-compatible CAD program for designing and drafting sewing patterns.

Garment Designer 2.5
PC- and Mac-compatible CAD program for designing and drafting sewing patterns.

USEFUL WEBSITES

Fashion Incubator
www.fashion-incubator.com
Networking and advice from industry professionals.

Flickr
www.flickr.com
Online photo-sharing and management application.

Grade House
www.gradehouse.co.uk
Grading and costing services.

Ponoko
www.ponoko.com
3D printing and laser-cutting "Personal Factory" facilitating the making and selling of custom products: think laser-cut accessories such as jewelry or buttons.

Spoonflower
www.spoonflower.com
Design and retail custom-printed fabric on demand with no minimum order.

Style.com
Style.com
Fashion news and trend reporting with extensive coverage of fashion shows.

RETAIL WEBSITES

ASOS
www.asos.com
Offers storefronts for vintage and fashion e-tailers.

Etsy
www.etsy.com
Handmade and vintage marketplace offering personal storefronts.

FashionStake
www.fashionstake.com
Online fashion boutique for professional independent designers.

Not Just a Label
notjustalabel.com
Showcase and retail platform for contemporary fashion.

FURTHER READING

Bray, Natalie, ***Dress Pattern Designing***
(John Wiley & Sons), 2003

Bray, Natalie, ***More Pattern Designing***
(John Wiley & Sons), 2003

Fasanella, Kathleen, ***The Entrepreneur's Guide to Sewn Product Manufacturing***
(Apparel Technical Services), 1998

Hagger, Ann, ***Pattern Cutting for Lingerie, Beachwear and Leisurewear***
(John Wiley & Sons), 2004

Nakamichi, Tomoko, ***Pattern Magic 1 & 2***
(Laurence King Publishing), 2010 & 2011

INDEX

ACKNOWLEDGMENTS

Jo and Andrew would like to extend huge appreciation to RotoVision, and to all those who have contributed to the book—in particular: Lindy Dunlop, Isheeta Mustafi, Emily Portnoi, Nicola Hodgson, and Rebecca Stephenson. A big thank you is also owed to our colleagues at Bath Spa University and City of Bath College, and to the designers Alexandra King and Feral Childe for their contributions.

Jo would like to give a big shout out to Mr. Freeman, Mrs. Skirty, Miss Leake, and, of course, Mr. Richards.

Andrew would also like to thank Lucinda, Jacky, and Jo.